HORSE TALES

HORSE TALES
True Stories from an Idaho Ranch

Heather Smith Thomas

Published by The Homestead Press, LLC

thehomesteadpress.com

CONTENTS

CONTENTS
CONTINUED

This book is dedicated to all the horses in my life, in gratitude for the good times they've given me and the many life lessons they've taught me.

PREFACE

When I was a small child, I wanted a horse. My family lived in town, but I dreamed of living on a ranch. When I was nine years old, my fondest wish came true; my parents helped me purchase my first horse – a sleepy old bay gelding named Possum.

But then we needed a place to keep the horse. That first summer, we kept Possum in a pasture on the edge of town. The next year we moved to a small acreage high in the mountains, along a little creek. A couple years later we moved to a ranch on that same creek. I spent the rest of my growing up with horses and cattle, and knew that this was the way I wanted to spend the rest of my life.

When my husband, Lynn, and I were married, we started buying the ranch from my parents, along with another ranch next to it. We still live on Withington Creek, 48 years later, raising cattle, enjoying our horses, and watching our grandchildren enjoy horses.

This book is about the horses in my life. They all had very different personalities and each one taught me a lot – not just about horses and riding, but about life and responsibility, patience, respect and trust, consistency and perseverance.

I have always enjoyed my horses and have been grateful for the many things they've taught me and keep teaching me. Our animals give us purpose and meaning for our lives as we try to take good care of them and be true to the trust they have in us.

POSSUM
A Wise Old Horse for a Beginner

I can't remember when I first fell in love with horses. My parents told me that before I could walk or talk, I looked at pictures of horses in storybooks. My favorite stuffed animal was a funny-looking, long-necked horse with a string mane. I called him "Shore-shay," the closest I could come to saying "horsie."

As a young kid, I spent much of my time playing with small plastic horses, making my own farms with tinker-toy corrals in our living room, or galloping herds of "wild horses" over the front lawn and my mom's flower beds. If my friends came to our house to play, we played with those toy horses, or sometimes pretended to be wild horses, snorting and galloping around the back yard, or we rode broom-handle stick horses, playing cowboy. I had a sleek black handle from an old janitor's mop; in my imagination, this was a fiery black steed with a long black mane and tail.

I wanted a real horse, but we lived in town – my dad was a Methodist preacher in Salmon, a small town in the mountains of central-eastern Idaho – and didn't have a place to keep one.

HORSE TALES

My dream seemed impossible, but I started saving all my pennies, nickels and dimes (allowance money) and birthday dollars from grandparents, in the hope I could someday buy a horse.

My parents probably wished I was more interested in practical things, like learning to cook or sew, or music lessons, but I preferred to spend as much time as possible outdoors. My father even bribed me, promising me a horse if I could learn to play the piano as well as my mom did. For a while I resigned myself to lessons, but my heart wasn't in it. I daydreamed about riding horses.

Finally, my father must have realized the piano would never be a serious interest for me. The spring I turned nine, in 1953, he started looking for a horse. Fred Kohl, a rancher at the bottom of a mountain behind town, agreed to pasture a horse for us. After looking at several horses, my father found one he felt was suitable for a child. He took me and my little brother to see it.

The horse's name was Possum, a name he might've earned because he was lazy and often pretended to be asleep. He was owned by a teenage girl who was buying a younger horse. Possum was a bay gelding with a white face and a blue eye surrounded by a white marking. He was calm and gentle and accustomed to being handled by children. He'd been retired from a riding stable in a larger town, purchased by a family with young children, resold when those children grew, and resold again. It would be hard to guess how many children had learned to ride on him.

It was also hard to tell how old Possum was. The present owners didn't know, and he was past the point at which his age could be estimated by looking at his teeth, but he was probably in his mid twenties. He was healthy and sound, though, and a safe mount for a nine-year-old girl.

Me and my brother, Rocky, riding Possum at the cabin in 1954.

Linda Jo Herndon, the teenager selling Possum, put on his bridle, and my dad boosted me onto the horse's broad back. He was mellow and wise, and just stood there – until Linda Jo told me I had to kick with my heels or slap him on the rump with the reins. I finally got him into a plodding walk, but I didn't care if he was slow and lazy. I was just happy to have a horse. It was love at first ride. I rode him slowly around the pasture, bareback, after instructions about how to pull on the reins to stop him, and how to make him turn right or left. It was wonderful to sit on a real live horse.

My dad paid $50 for Possum; I chipped in my life savings, $5.55. Dad bought a bridle at the saddle shop, adjusted the headstall to fit Possum, and I rode him out of the pasture and along the road, with my parents and brother following slowly in our car. I rode Possum two miles around the outskirts of town to

Mr. Kohl's pasture, Possum's new home.

Possum and I had an immediate understanding. I didn't care if he went slowly, or if he stopped to eat grass. I was just happy to be up there on his back. In return, the old horse took very good care of me. He wasn't phased by cars and trucks going by. In his long life, he had encountered many things and had been ridden by so many children that nothing bothered him. He was a perfect horse for a beginner like me.

Possum's pasture was about a mile from our house, but I hiked up there every day after school. At first, Mr. Kohl, helped me catch him. Possum didn't want to be caught and he'd kick up his heels and head for the far corner when he saw someone coming with a bridle. Mr. Kohl and I would corner him by the barn fence.

After a few days, I was able to catch Possum by myself. I was very patient and it didn't matter to me if there were a few moments (or even half an hour) of cat-and-mouse games before he allowed himself to be caught. I was never in a hurry, never got angry. I was in love with that horse. Maybe my lack of frustration had an effect. He realized I would just keep following him around, so he no longer trotted off when I came to ride him. Maybe because he had such easy work, he didn't mind the riding. I never rode him very fast, and our lazy sojourns around the edge of town and up the mountain were never strenuous, and I often let him stop to graze along the way. Possum began to look forward to our rides, coming to meet me at the gate.

The hardest part was bridling him. I was short and he was tall. If he held his head up high, I couldn't reach it. So I coaxed him to put his head down, giving him a handful of lush grass or alfalfa, which he loved. Then I could slip the bridle on. Clumps of alfalfa grew along the lane, and I'd pick some on my way to the pasture.

Getting on him was difficult, since I rode bareback. I was too short to reach up, grab his mane and swing on, like I'd seen bigger kids do, so I had to lead him to a gate, fence, stump or some other object I could climb on, then slip onto his back.

When school was out for summer, I'd usually spend entire days with Possum. I had to clean my room and wash dishes first, but then I could hurry to Mr. Kohl's place. I'd ride all morning, end up at our house for lunch (letting Possum graze in the back yard), then have Mom or Dad boost me back on so I could ride all afternoon.

Sometimes I rode with Diane Moser, my best friend and "twin cousin," born the same day as me. We rode double along the quiet back streets at the upper end of town, or in the hills beyond. Occasionally, we were adventuresome and took longer rides, like the time we rode past the far end of town to visit a friend who lived on a ranch. The biggest problem with extended excursions was finding a way to get back on Possum if we got off. One of us could boost the other one up, but then the second person had no way to get on, and had to walk until we found a fence or a makeshift mounting block.

Necessity is the mother of invention, and I figured out a way to get on Possum without a fence. He and I worked out a system. I'd lead him to a grassy area, and while he had his head down grazing, I straddled his neck, facing his withers. Then he'd raise his head and I'd slide and wiggle to his back, turning around to a mounted position.

Diane and I also worked out a way to take turns sitting in front. It was always more fun to be the "driver" – the person behind was merely a passenger – but to take turns, we had to switch places without getting off the horse, since it wasn't always easy to get back on. (Diane wasn't brave enough to try the get-on-the-neck trick.) So the person in front would scrunch down and scoot backward while the person behind would carefully go over the top of her and end up in front. Possum patiently stood still, so we could make a switch safely.

Possum was accustomed to children's antics and was a perfect babysitter. Sometimes I left him in the backyard at Diane's house and neighborhood children came to pet him, walk under his belly, or run up behind him while he was tied or grazing, and he didn't mind. He never spooked, kicked or bit. Even my mom finally quit worrying about the possibility of an accident.

The only "accident" that happened that summer occurred when there were no people around, and it taught me an important lesson. I occasionally rode with another young friend, Janet Meeks, who had a mare named Dolly. That hot afternoon, we had ridden for several hours and stopped at my house for some lemonade. We tied the horses by their bridle reins to an old power pole lying on the ground behind our garage, in the shade, next to the street.

The horses stood patiently for about an hour as we talked and rested in the house. Then we heard a loud bang and clatter. We rushed outside to check on the horses and found that the big pole had been pulled out into the street. The neighbor's garbage can was rolling down the street. Possum and Dolly were galloping away, heading downtown.

We ran after the horses and finally caught them. Dolly's bridle was broken, and I found Possum's headstall lying in the road with the metal bit bent and smashed where the power pole had rolled over it. I tied the broken reins around his neck to lead him home.

Something must have startled the horses, and they pulled backward. Since the pole was merely lying on the ground, it probably moved, rolling toward them and frightening them even more. So of course they tried to run away from it, and pulled it out into the road, knocking over the garbage can. The clatter probably made them pull even harder. They broke their bridles and ran off. My dad took Possum's bridle to the saddle shop to have Mr. Stone straighten the bit and mend the reins and headstall.

I learned a lesson that day. Never tie a horse by the bridle reins, and never tie to anything that might move. Possum got over his scare and was still well-mannered about being tied, but if this had happened to a younger, more nervous horse, this bad experience might have made the horse untrustworthy for tying in the future. I tried to never do anything that foolish again.

Having a horse in the family changed our lives. My dad had grown up on a farm near Rupert, Idaho, and enjoyed rural life. My parents wanted to find a place out of town, and now they had more incentive because we needed a place to keep our horse. That fall (1953) they found a little log cabin on seven acres for sale. It was 16 miles from town, up Withington Creek, in the bottom of a canyon. The next spring, we borrowed a horse trailer and took Possum up there, and lived in the cabin the next two summers when my little brother Rocky and I weren't in school.

There was no traffic on the little dirt road; the cabin was in the forest, above all the ranches. The little creek was cool and my brother and I spent happy hours playing in the water on hot afternoons. There was no electricity; our food was kept cool in waterproof containers in the creek, or in the old cellar dug into the mountain. We used candles and kerosene lanterns in the cabin at night, and a flashlight to go to the outhouse in the dark, always hoping we wouldn't meet a skunk or a bear.

When it rained a lot, the road was impassible. Several times that summer our car couldn't make it through the mud. We spent a day or two each weekend at our house (the church parsonage) in town, to go to church and do our shopping and laundry.

Mom took our weeks' worth of clothes to town, to wash in our electric washing machine. But when the road was too muddy to get clear up to the cabin, we had to park the car a couple miles below it, and hike up the road. When we came down later in the week we carried our laundry in a big duffel bag. But it was fun being isolated in our little cabin, in our own little world, up the creek.

The most fun was having new places to ride. Possum and I explored the jeep road up the canyon and into the mountains, but one time we went exploring too far. At the head of the canyon, up the left fork of the creek, was an old copper mine. I'd heard many tales about the Harmony mine but had never seen it. The mine was active during the 1920s and at one time the Chicago gangster Al Capone owned a major interest in it. The copper ore was hauled out in horse-drawn wagons.

One morning, Possum and I found ourselves at the fork of the creek and I decided to go up the left fork – which I'd never seen. The farther I went, the more I wondered about the abandoned mine, and thought we must be getting close. We kept climbing the steep, rutted jeep tracks, though it was nearly lunchtime by then and I knew Mom would be expecting me back at the cabin. But I'd gone so far, I surely must be almost there.

The Harmony mine was much farther up the canyon than I

expected, and it was afternoon by the time I reached the old mill building on the steep mountain. Farther up were old cabins, the cookhouse, and a steep road winding up through the timber to one of the mine tunnels. The mine hadn't been worked for years, but there were so many things left in and around the buildings that it looked like people lived there a short time ago.

After a quick look around, I rode back down the jeep road, hurrying because we were so late. Indeed, Mom was very worried when I didn't show up for lunch. She imagined all kinds of accidents, and since Dad was in town for the day, doing his work at the church office, Mom and my little brother started up the road on foot to look for me.

I met them at one of the creek crossings where the old log bridge had washed out; they were trying to get across the creek on logs and rocks without getting their feet wet. They were glad to see me, and after that, I tried not to worry my mother so much.

I got a dose of worry myself one day when we came back to the cabin after being in town for the weekend. Possum was gone. Fear clutched at my heart as I searched for him. There was a bad place in the fence by the creek, and horse tracks on the other side of the fence in the soft dirt. Possum had stepped over the fence, into a 320-acre mountain pasture belonging to the rancher who lived farther down the creek. I hiked and hiked, and finally found Possum grazing in a grassy meadow along the brushy creek bottom, about a quarter mile from our place. I put his halter on and rode him home.

~

HORSE TALES

It was a wonderful summer, living at the cabin. One highlight was a family reunion, when several aunts, uncles and cousins, as well as my grandma, Lila Moser, came to visit. She was past 70 and hadn't ridden a horse since she was a young girl, but the family talked her into getting on old Possum. Dad put his old saddle on the horse, and he and Mom and an uncle helped grandmother onto the horse, first helping her up onto our picnic table, from which she could step into the stirrup.

Once mounted, grandmother proudly rode Possum up and down the jeep track in front of the cabin. Possum walked slowly and carefully, and didn't even try to stop and eat grass along the way. It was as though he knew he had a fragile, precious passenger.

He was such a wise old horse. He would trot or gallop for an experienced rider (as I became a better rider, I loved to gallop him up a special place in the road that I called Possum's Hill). But if a small child or inexperienced person was on his back, he'd never go faster than a walk, and was careful to not get close to thorny rose briars or walk under a low-hanging tree branch. He took very good care of his inexperienced passengers.

The only time I ever saw him grumpy was when our cat, Thomas, kept rubbing on Possum's nose while he was trying to graze as I was brushing him. Finally Possum had enough of the tickly cat hair. He took hold of Thomas with his teeth, picking the cat up by the tail. Possum didn't bite hard enough to injure the cat; he just held him up in the air for a moment, yowling and clawing. The cat was unable to reach the horse with his claws, and eventually Possum set him down again. From then on, Thomas left Possum alone.

That summer we often ate meals outdoors, and my brother

Possum and I at the ranch in 1956.

and I discovered that Possum loved watermelon rinds. After awhile, however, he got fussier, and would only eat them if there was still a little bit of juicy red stuff left on the rind.

Possum was probably the wisest horse I ever had. Though I've owned and raised dozens of horses, none of them were quite the same as old Possum. He lived with us for the rest of his life. He became slower and stiffer in old age, but was still the perfect horse for any young or inexperienced visitors.

He was well past middle age when he became part of our family in 1953, but the six years we had him were wonderful. As my first horse, he gave me confidence and a lot of experience – lessons that would stay with me through the rest of my career with horses. By the time he died, we had several other horses, and a ranch, and I was living my dream – riding horses nearly every day, helping take care of cattle, and raising my first foal.

After spending two summers at the cabin up Withington Creek, my father went into partnership with his brother and borrowed money to buy the neighboring ranch when it came up for sale in 1955. He bought a small herd of Hereford cattle, and several more horses. Possum was one of our "work string" when we rode range to check or move cattle. He wasn't the fastest horse when we had to chase a cow, but he did his job. He went on hunting trips every fall; Dad used him to pack out a deer or elk for our winter's meat.

Old Possum was still healthy and strong through his final summer. We used him as a spare horse when we needed more riders to gather cattle, or when friends and relatives came to visit and wanted to ride. My mom, who had no horse experience and no desire to ride horses, overcame her timidity enough to ride Possum a few times; he was the only horse she felt was completely trustworthy. After my baby sister (12 years younger than me) was born, mom let me take her with me on Possum for short rides. By the time she was two, we let her sit in the saddle by herself as he grazed in the orchard. We knew he'd take good care of her and walk out around the low-hanging branches.

By contrast, Possum didn't have as much patience with riders who made him work hard. He did his job when he had to chase cattle or travel all day in the mountains, but he preferred to be ridden by children. On occasion, when we'd start out in the morning and Possum suspected it was going to be a long range ride or cattle roundup, he'd limp. Fearing he had a problem, his rider might take him back home. But miraculously, when heading home, the limp disappeared. We realized this must have been an old trick he'd used in the past, to get out of a hard day's work. If we didn't head back

Heading out to ride range in 1958 – my brother on Scrappy,
Dad on Possum, and me on Ginger.

home, he'd give up the lame act and do his job.

Possum's age caught up with him during the fall of 1959. His old joints became stiff and sore during cold weather and he had trouble getting up and down. We put him in the corral, where he could eat hay and not have to travel to feed and water, or compete with younger horses for food. Dad broke ice for him at the creek. Standing around, with little exercise, his hind legs began to swell. Our vet thought he was suffering from kidney failure and prescribed medication to put in his grain. One morning (November 12, 1959), Dad checked on Possum, after I had gone to school, and found the old horse lying down, unable to get up. The kindest thing to do was let him go.

I felt badly that I didn't have a chance to say goodbye, but I also knew it would have been cruel to let the old horse suffer any longer on the cold, frozen ground. I knew in my heart that my dad did the only humane thing. As a young horse owner, I learned that love is a two-way street. We love the creatures put into our care, but we also have a great responsibility to do what's best for them, in life and also when it comes time to end that life. I no longer had Possum, but I had all the good memories he left with me.

By then, I was in 4-H. In my 4-H scrapbook I drew sketches of my special old horse, and bade farewell to Possum, who started me along the road to good horsemanship. I found a poem that expressed my emotions, and copied it into my scrapbook:

A Parting

I love the earth your hoofs have pressed,
the far skyline your eyes caressed

The sunny days, the hills, the glades,
the wind-stirred trees, the rugged trails
Are all more beautiful to me because you lived life joyfully.

And as you go, as all must do,
I'll keep the truths I learned from you.

- author unknown

My dad wrote a poem about the hard task of love, releasing a beloved horse from the bonds of pain, and it was among a group of poems he later printed in a small pamphlet, *Ranchland Poems*, by Don Ian Smith.

Old Horse

Old faithful horse, I find you by the creek.
You try to stand but you are much too weak.
I know the end has come for you at last;
Too many times has winter come, and passed.
Too many times we've heard the blackbirds call
In spring; watched summer turn to fall.
And I have tried before with pills and grain
To get you on those ancient feet again.
But I can tell this time it cannot be.
It's in the way you moan and look at me.

You've been a great old horse, all I could ask.
You've never backed away from any task.
So many years have come to take their toll
Since first you were a bright-eyed little foal.
When you were young and strong you knew no fears
But now it's been so many, many years.
O God, I wonder why it has to be
This hard and lonely act is left to me?
Love leaves no choice as far as I can see
But quick and kindly death to set you free.

I'll get my gun down from the rifle rack.
Old friend, how many times you've had to pack
Some big old buck down off the steepest hill
When this same rifle made its smashing kill.

HORSE TALES

I'll blink away the salty, futile tears,
Forget a moment, all the pleasant years.
I could not stand the sense of foolish shame
I'd feel if blurring vision spoiled my aim.

It's hard for me to do this final task
And yet somehow I know it's all you ask.
I cannot leave you lying here to die
By inches, while impatient magpies fly
Around your drooping head. They will not wait
The dignity of death to seal your fate.
There's only one thing left for me to do,
And that's to send this bullet straight and true
To smash your aching, aged, weary brain
And cut the snubbing rope of age and pain
That keeps your poor old body firmly bound
To this one little spot of frozen ground.

O God, it's done… it's all that I could do!
I think I feel, God, how it must hurt you
When your love takes a mortal life away
To set a spirit free, to let it play
Once more out in the pasture of the sky
Where grass is always green and bluebirds fly.

NOSEY
The Horse We Won at the Grocery Store

When I was 11, during the second summer my family lived in the log cabin up Withington Creek, we unexpectedly became the owners of a second horse, one acquired under unusual circumstances.

My mom bought groceries in town, at a market owned by friends named Capps, who had a ranch along the Salmon River. That spring, they were giving away a palomino pony in a sales-promotion drawing at their store. Customers received tickets for the drawing when they made purchases. At the end of a certain month, the ticket stubs were put into a large bowl and the winning number was drawn. That number was posted in the store and mentioned in the local newspaper (this was before we had a radio station in Salmon), but no one ever came forth to claim the prize.

One day my mom was in the store and Mrs. Capps mentioned they still hadn't found the person with the winning ticket. Mom had all her ticket stubs in her purse, but she'd never looked at them. In truth, she wasn't interested in winning a horse. But she dug them out, and sure enough, she had the winning number.

The horse we won turned out to be a large buckskin mare named Nosey. The intended "palomino pony" had drowned while crossing the river that spring during high water, and Nosey was a substitute.

My dad borrowed a small, open-top trailer to bring our new horse home. Nosey was tall and skittish, and became nervous riding in the trailer. When it started bouncing on the rough little jeep track up to our cabin, Nosey got even more scared and tried to jump out. Fortunately, my dad was driving slowly and Nosey wasn't hurt when she leaped out of the trailer; she suffered only minor scrapes.

Her head was still tied to the front of the trailer, however, and she was hanging there by the halter, about to be strangled. My little brother Rocky and I were watching out the back window of our car and saw her jump out.

We yelled at Dad and he immediately stopped the car and we all jumped out and ran back to rescue Nosey. Rocky had a pocketknife, and Dad used it to cut the rope and free the mare. She stood there shaking and trembling, so we petted and talked to her, then let her eat grass along the road to help calm her. We didn't dare put her back into the trailer and risk having her try to jump out again, so I led her the rest of the way to our cabin, about half a mile.

Now old Possum had a buddy. When I turned Nosey loose into his pasture, the old lazy gelding suddenly came to life and chased the big mare around. I was upset, afraid he might hurt her, but my dad explained that horses have to establish a pecking order to determine who is boss. Dad said that once they figure it out, they'd get along fine. In a herd, there's always one horse who is boss, and the others stay out of his or her way, letting the boss drink first, or eat the best food. They all accept their place in the system, except when an aggressive younger horse moves up through the ranks and starts bossing some of the others.

My dad was right. After Possum and Nosey had their fight, and he chased her through the creek and bit her on the rump, they had it all settled. Possum was the boss and Nosey the meek follower. From then on, they were best friends. Possum had been very happy all those years living by himself, but now that he had Nosey, he wanted to be with her all the time; Nosey felt the same way. If we rode one horse, the other would whinny and run up and down the fence until the two were reunited.

Nosey was not as calm and gentle as old Possum. She'd grown up in the mountains and was surefooted and accustomed to wildlife, but not used to people. She didn't like to be caught, and was even more elusive than Possum had been when I first got him. I had to take a pan of grain out to the pasture to catch Nosey. Even then, she'd try to grab a bite of grain and jerk away. To catch her, I'd slip a rope around her neck, kind of sneaky-like, and then hold her there with the rope while I put the halter on. I didn't dare leave a halter on her as there was too much brush and other obstacles in the pasture that could catch a halter. I had to be patient to outsmart Nosey because she was often devious. One time, I reached around her neck to slip the rope around it, and she spun away. I grabbed her long, black mane, but Nosey whirled and bolted. I hung onto her mane for an instant as she whirled, swinging wildly through the air with my feet off the ground, then had to let go, rolling head over heels as the mare thundered away.

31

HORSE TALES

One day a few years later, after we had a ranch and the horses were in a much bigger pasture, Rocky and I wanted to ride both horses and didn't want to spend an hour trying to corner or outsmart Nosey, so we devised a plan to catch her quicker. I set the pan of grain in the trail and Rocky put a loop of rope (with a slipknot) on the ground by the pan. He took the other end of the rope and hid in the bushes behind a big tree, tying his end of the rope to the tree. I stood back, and called the horses.

Possum and Nosey came trotting down the trail. Seeing the pan of grain and no one close by to catch her, Nosey charged ahead to get to the grain first. As soon as one of her front feet was inside the loop of rope, Rocky pulled it tight with a jerk.

When the rope tightened around her front pastern, Nosey leaped backward, whirling around to gallop back up the trail. When she hit the end of the rope, Rocky's knots held, and the mare crashed to the ground. She almost did a somersault when her front leg was suddenly pulled out from under her. She got up and stood there, stunned and shaken, as I quietly walked up and put the halter on her.

Rocky and I were also a bit shaken. We hadn't realized the mare would hit the end of the rope that hard, and we were thankful she wasn't hurt. I don't think we told our parents about this misadventure until long afterward. Needless to say, we didn't try that method again. We resigned ourselves to being patient and trying to catch Nosey with grain and a halter.

In later years, the skittish mare became easier to catch, partly because I was always patient and took the time to out-wait her (as a child, I generally wasn't in as big a hurry as adults on a busy schedule), and partly because Nosey became more mellow and

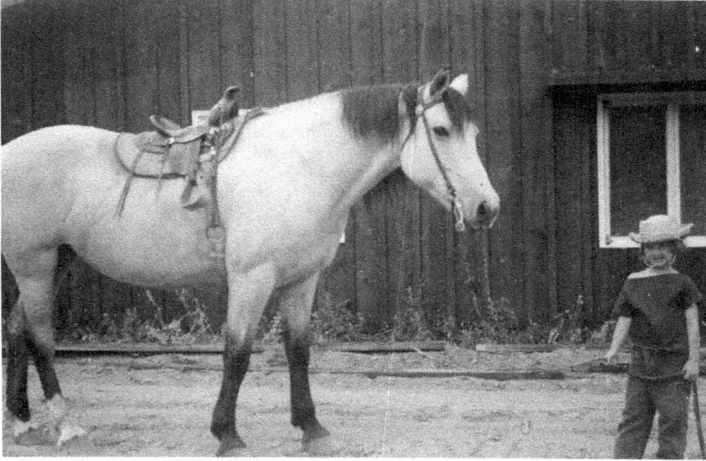

Nosey in 1961 with my little sister.

tolerant. In the meantime, however, we suddenly had several more horses, and I developed a good system for catching them all.

The ranch below our little cabin and pasture on Withington Creek was 640 acres, which included several small hay meadows and a lot of mountain pasture, providing feed for about 50 cows. My dad and his brother (an attorney in Idaho Falls, 170 miles away) went into partnership to buy the little ranch. My family took care of the ranch and the cattle, with my brother Rocky and me doing most of the irrigating and fencing since Dad still had his job in town, as preacher.

My uncle's interest in the ranch was mainly as an investment, and a place where he could bring his family to ride horses on summer weekends. My dad eventually traded for my uncle's share of the ranch, exchanging it for our little acreage and cabin (farther up the creek). The cabin was perfect for my uncle's family vacations.

I'd always dreamed of living on a ranch, with horses and cattle, and now we had more horses. A filly named Ginger came with the ranch, and we bought another yearling filly, a brown Thoroughbred named Nellace, from Lester Withington. Lester was an elderly cattleman who owned the ranch at the mouth of our creek, which was named for his grandfather, who homesteaded there.

Our ranch had few fences, except for the boundary fence around the half that lay along the creek. Another 320 acres in the mountains wasn't fenced at all. Near the old house, next to the creek, was a big corral where former owners kept their horses when they gathered them off the range, and a tall round corral for breaking horses. There were two sod-roofed sheds and an old wooden granary and milk house. Rocky and I helped dig postholes for a new fence to create a pasture above our house.

We also built a battery-operated electric fence to separate 70 acres of mountain pasture from the hay meadows. We let the horses run on the 70 acres in the hills up Cheney Creek (named for the family that homesteaded this ranch), to keep them out of the hayfields along the main creek. With that much area to roam, the horses were usually up on the mountain, and difficult to catch. Yet we needed them nearly every day to ride range and take care of the cattle. Dad purchased some Hereford cows and during the summer they were on BLM range and a long way from the ranch. The only way to check on them, move them or round them up in the fall was with horses. Riding range was one of my favorite things to do.

It was also my job (a delightful task) every morning to hike up Cheney Creek and find the horses. I took a small bucket of grain and a halter to catch old Possum. Even if the mares and fillies were flighty and hard to catch, Possum was still my buddy and he'd always come to me for grain, and didn't mind being caught. Then I'd get on him bareback. There was always a steep hillside that I could use for climbing onto him fairly easily while holding onto my grain bucket. Once mounted, I'd head down to the corral, calling the horses. They didn't want to be left behind, because Possum was their boss and leader, and they always followed him.

They knew there was a reward waiting for them in the corral, and they went galloping madly down the trail ahead of Possum and me. I had to become a good rider to stay on old Possum bareback, hanging onto his mane, the halter rope and the empty oat bucket as he galloped down the steep trail, following the mares through thick bushes.

Every day, before I hiked up Cheney Creek, I poured oats into feed boxes Dad built in the corral so that when the horses came galloping down the hill and into the corral, there would be a treat waiting for them. In a billow of dust they would pass me and Possum and dash to the feed boxes. I'd slip off old Possum and shut the gate, then turn him loose to let him go eat some of the oats. Once inside the corral, the horses were easier to catch, even Nosey. I could always corner them in the corral, and Nosey seemed to realize there was no point in trying to run away.

During one of the first corral episodes, however, she tried to evade capture. My dad was helping me catch her in the round corral and she kept running around us. He threw his lariat over her head but missed a perfect catch, his rope hanging by one ear. Nosey immediately stopped in her tracks, assuming she was caught, and we realized this must have been the way her former owner caught her.

~

Nosey became a useful ranch horse. She was much younger and more spirited than Possum, so I often rode her when I went up in the mountains to check on our cattle. In later years, she was a good "spare" horse for experienced riders. Our cousins enjoyed riding Nosey when they came to visit, and my baby sister started riding the big mare when she was about six years old, after she'd practiced for several years on old Possum.

Nosey was also a good pack horse. Dad bought a pack saddle, and used Nosey to pack blocks of salt to the range for the cows. When we repaired some of the old fences and started building new fences, we used Nosey to pack posts and heavy rolls of barbed wire up the steep hillsides.

One half-section of our ranch had no boundary fence. There had been a fence built around part of it when it was homesteaded in the early 1900s, but that old pole fence had fallen down and rotted away. Before we could use this part of our ranch for our cattle, we had to build a fence around it. At that point, it was grazed by all the neighbors' range cattle during the summer as part of the public range.

Rocky and I helped our dad and a cousin build the 2.5 miles of fence around that pasture (the half mile bordering another half section was already fenced). We dug post holes, set posts and tamped them, and stapled the wire after Dad strung it out along the posts, using Nosey to pull the wire. My brother and I kept hold of the metal bar the roll of wire was spinning on, and Dad rode along the fence line, with the end of the wire tied to his lariat, which was tied to the saddle horn. He and Nosy could string out the wire and drag it along the ground much easier than a person could, because often the wire got caught on sagebrush and it took strength to pull it free.

Nosey also packed the rolls of barbed wire to the top corners of the fence, where it was too steep to drive with the jeep. It was so steep that when Rocky and I were unloading two of the rolls, one fell back down the hill and we couldn't catch it. The heavy spool of wire went rolling and bouncing, faster and faster, with longer bounces, almost half a mile down the mountain before it came to rest in a flatter area in the tall sagebrush. We had to lead Nosey down there and lift that heavy roll back onto the pack saddle, then lead her up the mountain again.

It took us all summer and fall to finish that fence. We also built a fence around our orchard and garden by the house, so the horses and cattle couldn't get into the garden or chew on the apple trees. Dad paid us 50 cents an hour or 50 cents per post hole, whichever was more. In rocky terrain on the mountain pasture, we were glad to get 50 cents an hour, because it often took several hours to dig one hole. By contrast, we could make more money paid by the post hole in the rock-free soil around the garden, putting in several posts per hour, so we felt that was a good deal.

The most fun was riding in the mountains, checking cattle. There was a lot more territory out there than I'd ever explored on my earlier rides up the creek from our cabin. My brother, Rocky, and I learned where all the fences, gates and water troughs were. We learned the grazing habits of cattle and where we'd most likely find them.

That summer I needed a saddle for range riding, to make it easier to dismount and mount again as I opened and shut the wire gates. Nosey wasn't as patient as old Possum for getting on bareback, and was also much taller. I also needed a saddle so I could take a jacket (in case of thunderstorms) or my lunch. I could tie my jacket, lunch, or a hammer and sack of fence staples to my saddle.

I used a borrowed saddle from Lester Withington, one of the ranchers who had cattle on the same range. He was pleased that I was riding out there to help check the range. He sometimes rode with me, and showed me where the spring boxes for the water troughs were buried, since we sometimes had to open the top of a spring box and unplug the water line if a trough quit working. Occasionally a drowned mouse would get stuck in the pipe and we had to pull it out. I also helped Lester move cattle.

Then my dad bought me an old repaired saddle from Clyde Stone at the saddle shop. It had been used for roping, but the rear cinch had been torn out of it in some kind of accident. Mr. Stone repaired the saddle without adding a back cinch. It was less expensive than a new saddle, and he shortened the lace-up stirrup fenders, as short as they could go, since I was very small at age 12. I am still riding that same old saddle, 58 years later, with the same short stirrups.

With a saddle of my own, Rocky could use the borrowed saddle from Lester. Together, Rocky and I explored the range, riding Possum and Nosey, or the new black mare, named Scrappy, that our dad bought that summer, since our two fillies (Ginger and Nell) were still too young to be ridden.

When riding in our home pastures, however, we still rode bareback, especially after hiking to catch the horses. We'd gallop back to the barnyard, hanging onto a handful of mane. The horses loved to jump the irrigation ditch as we thundered toward home. But one time, when Rocky and Nosey got to the ditch and he was prepared for her to jump it, she suddenly stopped and he didn't, tumbling over her head into the water.

Nosey

Little sister Heidi riding Nosey in 1962.

Our cattle range had many interesting places to ride. The lower part was low hills and lots of sagebrush. A little stream, Baker Creek, ran though the range, but the lower end always dried up in late summer after weather turned hot. The top end in the mountains was fed by a series of little springs.

Much of the range was very steep. On one of our first rides on Possum and Nosey, Rocky and I were trying to go around a mountain to find Flicker Spring and a water trough we hadn't seen yet, following directions Dad gave us. We were supposed to go around the first big mountain beyond Baker Creek and then up a big draw. But we started up a false draw instead, before we got clear around the mountain. So we ended up climbing the steep mountain. The little draw we were following got steeper and soon there was no trail. We were halfway up the mountain by then, and it was so steep we were afraid to try to turn around and go back. It seemed safer to keep going up and angle over the top, and then go over into Baker Creek, where we knew our way around better.

The farther we went, however, the steeper it got. Soon we were in treacherous rocks with poor footing. Every rock dislodged by our horses' feet went crashing down the mountain. One big rock was immediately airborne and made only three bounces down to the flatter country below. The terrain was becoming more challenging, but it was still easier to keep climbing than try to go back down. Nosey slipped and her hind legs slid downhill several feet. The mare pulled herself back up by digging in with her front feet. We dismounted, leading the horses through the rocks the rest of the way to the top.

We were relieved when we got out of the rocks. We finally made our way back down the less-steep side of the mountain into Baker Creek. We'd had enough excitement for one day and decided to try to find Flicker Spring another time. After we got home and described our ride, Dad said that side of the mountain was "steeper than a cow's face!" From then on, that slope was called Cow Face by our family.

I was glad Nosey and Possum were strong and surefooted. If either of them had fallen, they'd have rolled all the way to the bottom. Nosey was a good mountain horse and didn't panic in precarious situations. Her surefootedness was a blessing.

Dad rode her on many hunting trips, leading a pack horse or string of pack horses when he went elk hunting in the backcountry with his friend Gene Powers. One time the pack horse he was leading slipped off a steep trail and might have tumbled to its death down the cliff, but Dad took a dally around his saddle horn

Cousin Jennifer Durham riding Nosey, and me on Khamette.

with the lead rope and Nosey pulled the scrambling pack horse back onto the trail.

Another time, Nosey's strength and agility came in handy when Rocky and I were riding up Cheney Creek and found a stray Hereford bull belonging to a rancher who lived several miles farther up the valley. The bull had come through our fence and was all by himself. We started toward him to herd him down to our corral, so the neighbor could come get him, but the bull charged at us. Rocky was closest, on Nosey, and as the bull charged at her, she started to spin away. The bull rammed her in the front of her chest, jamming one horn into her flesh, and picked her up with his head. She jerked free and galloped up the hillside. We were lucky he hit her in the front, instead of broadside, or his horns may have ripped into her belly and vital organs.

41

HORSE TALES

Rocky and I were alarmed by the bull's aggressiveness; we were accustomed to our own gentle Hereford bulls. We threw rocks at the bull from a safe spot higher on the hill, but he wouldn't go down toward the corral. He just stood there and shook his horns at us. So we gave up and rode home to tell Dad. When Dad and our neighbor Warren Gooch rode up there the next afternoon, with Gooch's stock dog, they didn't have much luck, either. The dog tried to nip the bull, but every time the dog snapped at the bull's nose, he got a horn instead. The dog gave up and ran home. Dad and Mr. Gooch rode back down to our fields and gathered some of our cows to take up Cheney Creek to put with the bull, and then they were able to herd them all down together to the corral.

Nosey was a good all-purpose ranch horse, except for her skittishness. My little sister rode her after starting on old Possum. I often took her riding with me on short rides, teaching her the basics of horsemanship. One windy day in early spring, I was glad we weren't far from home when Nosey spooked at something and whirled around. She left my sister on the ground and ran home. I was riding a young filly, Khamette, I'd raised from foalhood and was training. Khamette was not quite three years old and had never had an extra passenger aboard, but she stood still as I pulled my little sister up behind me, and gave her a ride home. Nosey was happily grazing in the barnyard when we got there, and hadn't even stepped on her bridle reins to break them.

Over the years, she was mostly dependable (skittish, but never tried to buck), and we were glad to have her. As a substitute for the "palomino pony" that we unexpectedly won at the grocery store, she turned out okay.

GINGER
The Orphan Filly Who Came with the Ranch

When my family moved to the ranch on Withington Creek in 1955, a chestnut yearling filly was part of the deal. Ginger was a friendly, inquisitive character, but also a bit spoiled. She'd been orphaned at birth, and raised on a bottle, so she was more like a big puppy dog instead of a horse.

Her mother was a part-Thoroughbred mare named Lady Larabee, who belonged to Pepper Witteborg, the teenage boy whose mother Ida was selling the ranch. When Pepper went off to college before Ginger was born, the old mare was turned out on the range with several other horses. Mr. Witteborg planned to bring her home the next spring before she foaled.

As the story was told to us by Ida Witteborg, her husband rode out on the range periodically to check on the little band of horses, and they were doing fine – fat and happy. It was a mild winter and the snow never got very deep.

Spring came, and Mr. Witteborg rode out to find Lady Larabee and bring her home. But when he found the herd of horses, the mare was not with them. He searched the surrounding hills and didn't find her. The next day, he and a neighbor rode out again to look for the mare.

At last they found her, lying behind the bushes in a sheltered draw. As they rode closer, they could see that she was dead. What a shame, since the old mare had been so close to foaling.

But wait! Something moved! Their horses were snorting as they approached the dead mare, and now they snorted even more. The men heard a pathetic little whinny. A tiny foal scrambled to its feet, from where it had been lying on the other side of the mare, out of the wind. Upon hearing the other horses, the foal had gotten up, and came wobbling toward them, hungry and weak.

Mr. Witteborg got off his horse and the little filly came right up to him and nuzzled his arm, trying to suck his sleeve. Lady Larabee hadn't been dead very long. He hoped the foal had been able to nurse the mare before she died, but he wasn't sure. He gathered the foal in his arms, and carried it toward his horse. The horse jumped around as he approached, but his friend held the horse steady while Mr. Witteborg lifted the wiggling foal up across the saddle and mounted the skittish horse. He and his friend rode home, with the foal balanced across Mr. Witteborg's lap.

Ida heated some milk on the wood stove. They tried to get the foal to suck a bottle, but the foal refused. So Ida squirted some of the warm milk into the back of the foal's mouth with an eye-dropper. She fed the foal about a half cup of milk with the eye-dropper, a little at a time.

By the next feeding, the foal was a little stronger and more eager, and sucked the bottle. Ida named her Ginger because of her golden chestnut color. They made a place for her in one of the sod-roofed sheds. Eventually she lived in the orchard pasture with the ranch horses, and Ida bottle-fed the filly. Ginger became so attached to her human "mothers" that she wasn't very interested in the other horses; she preferred to spend time with people. She often followed Ida up onto the porch and tried to go into the house.

Ginger was a big sassy yearling in 1955 when we came to the ranch. Ida told us about the filly's background, which explained why she liked to follow us around and come into the house yard. She was pushy and spoiled, but also very trusting, like the time I walked through the orchard and Ginger came limping up to me, wanting me to take a rock out of her foot. It was wedged tightly, but she stood patiently as I picked up her foot and pulled and pried and finally got the rock out.

She made a nuisance of herself in the barnyard, however, always getting in the way, always chewing on everything, always getting into trouble. My dad decided Ginger should live in the pasture up Cheney Creek with our other horses. At first Ginger was unhappy about being banished from the orchard and barnyard. But soon she adapted to her new status and stayed with the little group of horses – Old Possum, Nosey, Scrappy and a two-year-old filly named Nellace.

I wanted to train Ginger to ride, but Dad didn't think that was a good idea. Because Ginger was spoiled and headstrong, Dad felt she might be too much challenge for an inexperienced 13-year-old girl to train. Ginger was gentle and would probably never buck, but she was stubborn and liked to have her own way – and might be a difficult pupil for someone who had never trained a horse.

So my father asked the neighboring rancher, Mr. Gooch, to start Ginger. He took her down to his place for a couple of weeks and got her used to wearing a saddle and bridle, and rode her every day – teaching her to stop, move out, and turn. He had to be firm with her at first, but she was smart and soon figured things out.

After those two weeks of "kindergarten," Ginger was more ready for me to start riding her. The filly was bold and not afraid of anything, and soon I was riding her out into the hills every day to check cattle. Ginger had a fast trot, and I enjoyed riding her.

I rode her so much that summer that her feet got tender and she needed shoes. Dad always put the shoes on our other horses, but he thought it would be good to have a horseshoer put Ginger's first set of shoes on.

Dad wasn't home when the shoer came. I haltered Ginger and brought her to the barnyard. Being timid, I didn't speak up when he tied her to the crosspiece on our big pole gate by the barn. She was fairly well halter-trained by then; we'd tied her up many times. But I worried about tying her to something that flimsy, especially for her first shoeing. I would have been glad to hold her instead, but the horseshoer was an old cowboy who didn't think a little girl could be much help.

Ginger was nervous about the shoeing and moved around a little. The shoer became impatient and slapped her for not standing still. This upset Ginger even more, and she pulled backward. The cross pole on the gate came loose. The filly went flying backward and the pole came with her, scaring her out of her wits. She went galloping around the barnyard with that pole chasing and bumping her. It took awhile before we could corner her and slow her down enough to grab her – so the pole would quit chasing her, so we could get it loose from her halter rope.

Ginger in 1956 – our first summer at the ranch.

After that traumatic experience, Ginger was never trustworthy to tie. She might stand calmly, or she might not – and whenever she set back, she did it with all her strength and determination. From then on, we tried to avoid situations where she'd have to be tied, to minimize the risk for broken halters and ropes, or injury to her neck.

In 1958, when I was in eighth grade, Jerry and Velma Ravndal, a ranch couple who had lived on an isolated ranch on the North Fork of the Salmon River, moved to a smaller ranch closer to town to raise Arabian horses, and started the first 4-H horse club in Idaho. I was part of their first crop of 4-H kids. About 25 of us (ages nine through 14) met at their home for meetings, and I decided to use Ginger as my project.

It was late winter and the weather wasn't nice enough yet to bring our horses. So the first meetings were spent learning about horse breeds, proper horse terminology, basic horse care and good horsemanship. We did a lot of reading and studying so we could take better care of our horses as well as learn how to become better riders.

We learned the proper ways to groom, catch and halter a horse; how to properly saddle and bridle our horses; how to tie them; the safest, correct ways to mount and dismount; and how to ride in balance with our horses at various gaits. The goal was to improve our communication with the horse, and our knowledge about feeding and health care. Many of the things covered in those first lessons I already knew because I'd read everything about horses that I could find in our local library. But there were still many important things I didn't know.

We called ourselves the 5-H Wranglers. The fifth H stood for horses. We held our summer meetings at the fairgrounds on the edge of town. Most of the members lived in or near town and didn't have very far to ride, but Ginger and I had 14 miles. My mom thought that was too far, but Ginger had a fast trot and I knew we could easily make it in a couple of hours. We could trot along the edge of the road where the ground was soft (not so hard on her feet and legs).

I wasn't sure how Ginger would react to cars whizzing by on the highway, since she'd never seen a highway before. Back in those days there wasn't much traffic, and I always rode facing the traffic because she was not as scared of cars and trucks if she could see them coming. She was more skittish if they came zooming up behind her. The big, noisy trucks were her worst problem and she'd try to spin away and bolt. If the truck was coming from behind us,

I had to turn her around so she could watch until it went by. She'd stand there trembling, but I could keep her from bolting.

The only time a scary truck nearly caused an accident was when my brother was riding Ginger to town the next year – when we were both in 4-H and I was riding Nell, one of our other ranch horses. As the truck approached, Rocky noticed that his cinch was loose. Ginger had a very round back – not enough withers to hold a saddle very well – so we always had to keep the cinch snug. Rocky realized that if Ginger tried to whirl away from the truck, his saddle would slip sideways. So he quickly jumped off and held her until the truck passed, then tightened his cinch before we continued on our way.

Ginger had a very fast trot. I timed her by the mile markers and found that her medium trot could cover a mile in 10 minutes and her fast trot was a mile in 4½ minutes. I became better at judging distances and speed, and as Ginger got in better shape we could make it to town in about 1½ hours, alternately walking and trotting. It took a little longer coming home in the afternoons. If it was really hot we didn't trot as fast.

That summer was glorious for a horse-crazy kid. Velma was a perfectionist about good horsemanship and our advanced group soaked it in. We learned how to handle our horses properly on the ground when leading them, how to teach them to walk faster when we were riding, how to post the trot, how to change leads at a gallop, how to "collect" our horses so they could move with more precision and agility when changing direction.

Our meetings were mostly lessons and hard work, but now and then the Ravndals took time for some "fun" rides, too, like the day we went on a trail ride into the foothills behind their ranch.

HORSE TALES

We took our lunches and had a picnic out on the trail.

As we came to the end of our summer's work, we were proud of our progress and accomplishments. The beginners were no longer bouncing at the trot or inadvertently jerking their horses in the mouth. Everyone was riding in balance with their horses' movements, and the horses were responding better to leg and rein cues. Horse and rider were becoming truly a team, working together in harmony and unison.

We put on a horse show for our parents, friends, and the community. We wore white shirts with green neckerchiefs, and dark colored pants, so we all matched. We cleaned our saddles, washed our saddle blankets and had our horses neatly groomed. During the show we gave demonstrations on correct methods of tying, leading, saddling and bridling, and had horsemanship classes to test our riding skills and our horses' training. The advanced riders demonstrated figure-eights at the canter, mounting and dismounting, and backing up.

Special events included a costume class, judged in pairs. My friend Marilyn Muench and I spent hours making Indian costumes, using burlap dyed brown, decorated with painted seashells, beads and feathers we sewed onto the burlap. We practiced riding our horses bareback with jaw ropes (no bridles).

Ginger was trustworthy for this kind of fun. She was tolerant of many things that a more nervous, flighty horse might not be able to handle. By that time I was tall enough (and Ginger was short enough) that I could mount her bareback by grabbing her mane and swinging a leg up over her back.

Marilyn's horse, "Sweetheart," was also gentle and we didn't have any trouble riding our steeds in the costume class, walking, trotting and cantering as a matched pair, controlling our horses with just a rope through their mouths.

The next summer my brother was old enough to be in 4-H and our parents thought he should use Ginger. At first I didn't want to give up Ginger because I enjoyed riding her so much, and I thought he should use Nosey (the big buckskin mare). But Nosey was very tall for a small boy, and more nervous than Ginger. Possum, my first horse, was too old and stiff for trotting back and forth from town. My dad talked me into taking our other young mare, Nell, as my project, so Rocky could ride Ginger.

So that summer we rode to town twice a week on Ginger and Nell for meetings and drill practice; the 5-H Wranglers were putting on a mounted drill for our horse show and for the fair. The two mares were in excellent condition, making the 28-mile round trip to town two days each week and riding range in between to check cattle.

Ginger was the reason I learned how to shoe. One week our parents were gone to a church conference in Montana and Rocky and I were taking care of the ranch. On one of our rides to move cattle, Ginger lost a shoe. She made it home without getting tender, but I knew she wouldn't be able to travel 28 miles the next day (on gravel roads and rocks) to our 5-H meeting without becoming sore.

We had a pile of old horseshoes in the shed – the worn-out shoes that had been taken off our horses over several years – and we searched though those. I found some shoes that Dad had taken off Ginger the year before that still had some wear left. They were the proper size and already shaped to her feet.

I got Dad's shoeing tools and horseshoe nails, and bravely tried my first attempt at putting a shoe on, while Rocky held Ginger. Her foot didn't need much trimming because she'd worn it off a bit after losing the shoe. Fortunately the hoof hadn't chipped. I smoothed it a little with the rasp and then placed the shoe as perfectly as I could.

Driving the first nail was the challenge, because I wasn't sure which way it should go. Horseshoe nails are beveled with a taper on one side of the tip, so they curve outward when driven – to come out the side of the hoof wall (¾ inch to 1 inch above the shoe) instead of going straight into the foot. I knew that if I placed the nail incorrectly, it would curve into the sensitive inner tissues and make her lame. I pounded it in a little ways, very carefully, and when it didn't start to come out, I pulled it out with the hammer claws, and set it the opposite way.

The nail started to poke out through the side of the hoof before I had it driven halfway, so I knew I had it right. I then realized that the nail heads were a clue; one side was smooth and the other was rough – probably so a person could tell by look and by feel which way the nail should go. Thus I learned my first lesson about horseshoe nails: rough side inside.

I made sure the shoe was still in proper position on Ginger's foot, and drove the other seven nails, twisting off the protruding tips with the hammer claws. Then I clinched them, the way I'd watched my father do it, using a piece of iron against the foot to make the nails turn over tightly as I pounded them a bit more.

I got that shoe on, and it stayed on through our trip to the fairgrounds and back the next day. When our parents got home later that week, Dad looked at Ginger's foot and thought I'd done a good job. After that, he let me shoe our ranch horses.

I've been doing it ever since (for more than 57 years). Dad gave me some advice that first year, and so did Jerry Ravndal. Jerry was an excellent farrier, and guided me through a "horseshoeing apprenticeship" as one of my 4-H projects.

Rocky and I made many trips to town with our horses and it was often hot in the afternoons on our way home. We stopped at the Baker Store, the little country store at the highway junction where we turned off the highway to go up Withington Creek. Mr. Crooks was always friendly and on hot afternoons he'd bring each of us a glass of water.

On really hot days we also stopped on our way in and out of town at the Arctic Circle, near the fairgrounds. This drive-in store sold milkshakes and ice cream cones. We didn't have money to buy anything, but used the water fountain in the parking lot. Ginger quickly figured out how to get a drink, too. When Rocky tried to get a drink she pushed him out of the way with her nose and sipped the water. So we'd always turn the water on for her and let her drink from the fountain. People passing by would stop and gawk at the horse delicately sipping water. Nell wouldn't try it, but Ginger looked forward to these water stops as much as Rocky and I did.

Even though my brother used Ginger as his 4-H project for several years, I still enjoyed riding her at home on the ranch. She was still my favorite horse for riding range until I became more at ease with riding Nell, the skittish Thoroughbred mare. Ginger was also the horse I rode for irrigating. Our little ranch had several hayfields, which we cut for hay once a year, baling and stacking hay for winter feed for the cattle and horses. Hayfields in our dry part of the West have to be irrigated. Our fields had to be watered with ditches, bringing water from the creek, and letting the water flood over the fields. Part of my summer job was to make sure there was enough water in each ditch, and to change the water every day. It usually took about a day for the water to run through on one "set." It might take a couple weeks to completely water a field from one end to the other, and then we'd start over again. There were several fields along the creek, each watered by a different ditch.

Every morning I'd ride to the upper end of our ranch and back, changing the water along the way. I usually rode Ginger because she was so calm about carrying a shovel and a canvas dam. I'd stick my shovel into the ground so that it stood upright, get on my horse, ride up to the shovel and grab it, then carry it over my shoulder as I rode from field to field. Some of the ditches were large and deep, and the only way to get the water dammed off enough to go out the irrigation slot was to use a canvas dam attached to a pole. The pole went across the ditch, and I could anchor the canvass with rocks in the bottom of the ditch to keep it in place.

Many horses might be a skittish about carrying a big canvas dam, even when it was all rolled up on the pole, but Ginger was at ease with everything I did with her. I usually leaned the rolled-up dam against a tree or a fence so I could get hold of it from horseback, then laid it across my lap against the front of the saddle, to carry it. Ginger didn't mind the cumbersome pole, even when it bumped into bushes we rode through.

She'd graze nearby while I changed the water, and never tried to run home. I didn't have to tie her, like some of our other horses that were always too eager to get back to their herdmates. Along

Ginger and me in 1958.

some of the ditches there weren't any trees to tie to, so it was much handier to ride Ginger instead. I'd tie her reins to the saddle horn so she wouldn't step on them, and let her graze.

Ginger was also good at herding cattle and chasing strays back to the herd when we took cattle out to summer range or moved them to a different pasture. She and I had become a really good team. The longest drive was in late summer, when all the ranchers on our BLM allotment met early in the morning and gathered cattle off the lower part of the range to take them up into the mountains where the grass was still green. We started early because we knew it would get hot and the cattle would have trouble climbing up the mountains in the heat.

Dad and I, riding Nell and Ginger, helped gather cattle out of the area around lower Baker Creek to start the long drive up to the head of Baker Creek and over the mountain into the right fork of Withington Creek. There were eight riders on that first drive, but it was still a difficult job to move all the cattle in one big herd up over a mountain where some of them had never been before.

By late morning we had them partway up Baker Creek, and stopped in the shade of the timber to let the horses and cattle rest, and to eat our lunch. After lunch we started the hardest part, pushing the cattle over the top of the mountain. The cows and calves were hot and didn't want to climb. Some kept drifting too far down the slope as we edged around the mountain, and I nearly wore Ginger out trotting and galloping back and forth on the lower edge of the herd, trying to keep cattle at the proper level, and keep the herd leaders moving upward instead of down.

It was the hardest work Ginger had ever done. Several riders were following the big herd, urging the cattle on, wearing handkerchiefs over their faces to keep from breathing too much dust. The rest of us were very busy along the lower edge of the herd, trying to keep the cattle moving upward.

If a cow or calf broke from the herd and started down the steep slope through the rocks, one of the cowdogs would usually chase it back, but some of the cows were cranky and tired and wouldn't obey the dogs, and a rider would have to go down after them.

Lester Withington was helping me work the downhill edge of the herd, using his bullwhip. The popping sound kept the cows moving in the proper direction. But after several hours of this effort, his arm got tired and he showed me how to swing the whip and pop it. I used his bullwhip until we got the cattle over the top and started down the other side into Withington Creek.

The cattle were tired, but they traveled much better going

downhill – and could smell the water ahead. When they got down into the meadow they all headed into the creek to get a drink. We went to the creek, upstream from the cattle, to drink and water our horses. I flopped down on my belly and sipped cold water from a small pool where it ran between some rocks. Ginger drank greedily, but I limited her to 15 swallows at first, because she was so hot and sweaty and I didn't want her to get stomach cramps and colic.

We let the cattle scatter out and graze, helping the bawling calves find their mothers. The cows were so busy eating the green grass that they weren't worried about their calves, and we had to make sure they "mothered up." If a calf doesn't know where its mother is, it will go back to the last place it nursed her. We didn't want any of those calves hiking back over the mountain in search of their mothers.

When we were sure they'd all found each other, we rode home down the little jeep road, letting our horses have a few more drinks each time the road crossed the creek – after they started to cool off. By the time Dad and I got home, we'd been riding for 12 hours. In later years, that wasn't an unusual thing, but at that stage in my young life it was the longest and most challenging ride I'd ever experienced. I was proud of Ginger for handling it so well.

She was a good cow horse, and always willing to work. In the winter we didn't ride much, and most of the horses got a vacation. Ginger was usually the one we'd grab if we had to do an unexpected cattle roundup – because she was always easy to catch, and level-headed. She wasn't silly after time off from work.

So she was the horse I chose one spring day in 1960 when my father and brother and I had to bring a cow into the corral to treat for a medical problem. I jumped on Ginger bareback to herd the cow in from the field. After we treated the cow, Dad and Rocky were putting equipment away and I rode Ginger for a few minutes around the pasture, practicing figure-eights at a canter. It was a lovely warm day and the ground seemed dry. I wasn't thinking about the fact it had been muddy not long before, and in some places the dirt was just dry on top.

Ginger hit a slick spot as she leaned into a tight turn at the canter, and her feet slid out from under her. She fell flat on the ground, and I didn't have time to jump clear or pull my leg out from underneath her. I wasn't wearing cowboy boots, and wasn't using a saddle, and there was nothing between my leg and her – and the ground. She smashed my ankle and broke it. To date, that's the only broken bone I've ever suffered – through various crazy adventures, spills and horse accidents.

My leg was in a cast for six weeks, and I was terribly upset about not being able to ride. I was afraid I wouldn't get the cast off in time for the special performance our 5-H Wranglers put on. I'd sold a story about our horse club to *Farm Journal* magazine and they were sending a photographer to take pictures. Fortunately my cast was off, in the nick of time, and I didn't have to appear on the cover of that magazine with a broken leg!

NELL
The Mare Who Taught Me the Most

When my family started ranching I was 12 years old, in sixth grade. Ginger, a sorrel filly, came with the ranch. Then we bought a brown Thoroughbred filly named Nellace from the old rancher down the creek.

The next year, I joined a new 4-H club – the first 4-H horse club in our state – and used Ginger as my project. She was mellow and easy to work with. Nell hadn't been handled much and was nervous and skittish so Dad sent her to be started by a horse breaker. Dad and I were inexperienced in horse training. His experience had been with teams of work horses he drove as a boy on his parents' farm in southern Idaho, and I'd learned to ride by trial and error, reading everything horse-related that I could find.

The man who broke Nell was not a trainer in the true sense of the word. Some horses can be treated the rough-handed way he rode Nell, and maybe turn out ok, but not her. She came back broke to ride but scared, sulky and resentful of humans. Dad rode her with caution. My uncle rode her and got bucked off.

HORSE TALES

She was sensitive and proud, with a lot of heart and spirit. If someone abused her, she fought back. Her basic disposition had been friendly, alert and inquisitive – but her bad start with the rodeo cowboy got her off on the wrong foot with humans. She was intelligent, fast, agile and quick as a cat. You had to be a good rider to stay topside when she was working cows or spooking; she could leap across the road and be heading the opposite direction in the blink of an eye.

Yet she was cool-headed for a Thoroughbred. Her sire, Cheyenne Chief, had a calm temperament. He was a Cavalry remount stallion, and the rancher who stood him at stud always ran him in the races at our county fair (winning them) and the same afternoon used Chief as a pickup horse in the rodeo arena. It takes a calm, sane horse to do that. Nell inherited her speed from him, too. Chief's sire, Pillary, won the Belmont Stakes and the Preakness in 1922 and was the top money-winning Thoroughbred that year. He didn't win the Triple Crown however, because he had not been entered in the Kentucky Derby.

My second year in 4-H, my younger brother joined the club and needed a horse to ride. Dad talked me into taking Nell for my project and letting Rocky ride Ginger. I was reluctant at first, because I was a little afraid of Nell. She was four years old then, still sulky, still carrying fierce resentment from her breaking experience. She was hard to catch, and kicked me on the leg one time when I tried to corner her in our corral. She tolerated me sometimes and other times she'd outright let me know that she'd rather I just leave her alone. Once I tried to stroke her neck after I caught her and she nipped me on the cheek. That hurt my feelings because I wanted to be friends with her.

Rocky and I rode range nearly every day to check cattle, and rode to town twice a week that summer to 4-H meetings at the fairgrounds – a 28-mile round trip. Nell usually settled down after about the first eight miles, but was sulky or skittish when starting a ride.

The first few times I rode her that spring, we had some arguments in the barnyard, because she didn't want to be ridden, but by then I was a good enough rider to stick with her and I could keep her from bucking. But she went over backward with me twice that spring during conflicts in the barnyard. Somehow I managed to jump clear. The second time, she just lay on the ground sulking, and my dad had to whip her to make her get up. Mom was worried about my safety and didn't want me to ride that mare again, but I swallowed my fear and got back on. As summer passed, we cautiously felt each other out and got along a little better.

Nell was feisty and spirited, and kept me constantly on my toes. Riding her did more than anything else to make me a better rider. I learned to become more sensitive to my horse. I treated her decently and she began to respond. We made some long journeys and difficult rides in steep country, riding range and moving cattle all day, but I never abused her. I lost my fear and gained a deep and lasting respect for her ability and judgment. She had a wonderful agility, handling herself in rough country; she never once stumbled or fell with me, in all our years of hard riding. I learned to trust her judgment in choosing the best way to go through precarious footing at top speed, and her ability to outrun and outmaneuver any bovine. I marveled at her courage and stamina.

We went through a lot together and she began to accept me. At last, we became a team. This means so much. When a horse gives you everything she's got, doing a hard job, all you can do is humbly appreciate it and be grateful. This didn't happen overnight, however. Her acceptance of me, and her willingness to work her heart out for me, was a gradual thing that took several years. How happy I was when she finally tolerated me enough to let me catch her. She still didn't come up to me like most of the other horses, but she'd stand and let me walk up to her, no longer trying to avoid me.

She was my 4-H project from eighth grade through high school and we did well at the county fair and all the open horse show classes. Our teamwork paid off and we usually placed in every event we entered. Our first bareback class was spur-of-the-moment; I'd never ridden her bareback. I'd been afraid to, because she was so quick and catty. But we entered, and came out with the blue ribbon.

The first year I rode her as my 4-H project, my brother and I rode Ginger and Nell to town for the Fair. We sat on our horses watching the other classes while we waited for ours. When it was time for the 4-H judging, we all rode our horses into the arena single file and made a big circle. The judge stood in the center and gave his instructions for us – to walk, trot, canter, stop – watching to see if horse and rider moved in harmony, whether the horse responded smoothly and easily to the rider's cues.

Then each of us had to perform individually, cantering away from the lineup and walking calmly back. A horse that didn't willingly leave the group, or pranced back instead of walking quietly, lost points. We had to back up, mount and dismount (and the horse was supposed to stand still), and then do a figure-eight at the walk, trot and canter.

When my turn came, I cantered Nell to the far end of the

Nell in 1961.

arena. She was moving freely, and I began to relax. If I could just keep my mind at ease, like when we were cantering after a cow on the range, instead of being so nervous! Nell made a nice square stop, and I spun her around and walked back to the group. Another nice stop, and I backed her up. Nell opened her mouth a little when I gave her the signal with my reins to stop – a habit she'd had ever since the horse breaker injured her mouth while fighting with her – but she performed well otherwise. She also stood quietly for me to dismount and mount. Nell's figure-eights at the trot (with me changing posting diagonals at each change of direction) and at the canter (changing leads with each new circle) went smoothly, and I felt like we'd both done our very best.

I was glad for all the hours I'd spent working with Nell, gaining her confidence and trust. This was a totally different Nell than the mare who resisted me so much at the beginning of our relationship.

My heart was bursting with joy at our accomplishments.

We had a bond that words can't describe, and anyone who has been privileged to ride a really good horse knows what I felt. But the thing that really cemented the bond between us occurred a year later, in 1960 when she suffered a tragic injury. Nell was seven years old and carrying her first foal. We'd bred her to El Khamis — my 4-H leader's Arabian stallion — a versatile little horse that packed deer during hunting season, worked cattle, and kept a rope tight to hold calves by himself after they were roped off him for branding. The eagerly-awaited foal was to be my next 4-H project.

In March, Nell jumped a barbed-wire fence and got caught in it, cutting her left front foot just above the hoof. It was a deep cut and I treated it every day after school for many weeks. She had the foal in May — a nice colt that I named Amahl (after the little boy in the Christmas opera Amahl and the Night Visitors) — but we lost him at a month of age, from complications following castration.

Our vet came out to the ranch to geld the little colt. In a foal, the testicles and blood vessels are small, with less risk for bleeding or extensive swelling afterward, and the foal has mama for comfort and companionship after the surgery and gets plenty of exercise following her around. There's no need for forced exercise like you'd do with an older animal to keep the surgical site open and draining and to minimize swelling.

But Amahl had a scrotal hernia — a separation in the muscle wall between the abdomen and the scrotum. This is uncommon, but tends to be hereditary, and I knew that El Khamis had sired a couple of foals with this problem. It's no big deal, as long as the veterinarian puts in a stitch or two to close that separation.

Being a shy child, and not one to question my elders, I wanted to ask the vet to check for a hernia, but was afraid to say anything. The surgery was quick and the vet put away his instruments, got into his little Volkswagen and headed back to town. Amahl was recuperating, out in the pasture, with mama standing over him.

I walked out there again, after the vet left, to check on my foal, and found him thrashing on the ground with his intestines coming out of the incision. I yelled for my dad, and we stayed with the foal, kneeling on the ground to hold him still, using a towel against the wad of intestines – to try to keep them clean, and prevent more coming out. Mom got in our car and hurried to town to try to catch up with the vet, because we didn't have a telephone at the ranch.

The vet came back, washed up the intestines, poked them back through the hole, and sewed up the incision. But Amahl never recovered from the trauma. I stayed all night in the corral with him and Nell, but he went into shock and grew weaker.

My parents had gone back to town that evening for a meeting, and stayed in our house in town that night (this was before we were living full time at the ranch). At 4 a.m. I became worried about Amahl's unresponsiveness, and I woke my brother. He rushed off to town in the jeep to call the vet, but little Amahl died in my arms before the vet could get there. Poor Nell stood over us, worried about her baby. After he died and she nuzzled the body, she knew it wasn't her baby anymore. She wandered around the corral and whinnied, making a sound I'd never heard before, and it tore my heart out. Horses truly do grieve. Then she came back to me and nudged me with her head, as if to ask for comfort for her lost baby.

~

Her injured foot was still mending. The wound developed proud flesh (overgrowth of granulation tissue, protruding out of the wound) and I treated it twice a day – a challenging ordeal. Back then we didn't know about better ways to prevent and treat proud flesh, and traditional treatments were harsh; scrub and pick off the scabs and apply a caustic agent to eat away the over-growing tissue. I spent hours doctoring that mare, and through it all we developed a bond of trust and respect that was deeper than I've ever had with any other horse.

Nell taught me patience and consideration. If I was in a hurry or became frustrated because of her nervous avoidance of the hurtful medication, she wouldn't let me handle the foot at all. At first, with my dad helping me, we tried various methods of restraint. There were ropes and harsh words and exasperated failures. But by mid-summer I was treating her without any fuss. I had to discard the attempts at restraint, and put aside my fear of her stomping or kicking. I had to just calmly get right down under her feet and trust her – and she finally came to trust me. From that point on I could walk up to her anywhere in the pasture and work on that foot, and she'd stand there quietly and let me do it. And the foot was looking better; we were making progress.

While she was lame, I rode one of our other ranch mares (Scrappy) to 4-H. That summer some of us in the 4-H club were studying dressage. We borrowed English saddles, and practiced dressage movements. I rode one of Ravndal's horses all summer in class because Scrappy was a gaited mare, unable to trot (she did a singlefoot instead), but I had my heart set on using Nell for the final test at the fair.

It was late summer when I finally began riding her again, after

Nell and her second foal, Nikki, newborn, in 1962.

she was no longer lame. I rode her for short periods because she was out of shape and her injured tendon was badly shortened. I was still treating the foot daily. We gradually built up the strength of that tendon, riding 10 minutes at first, then 20, then 30, stretching the tendon, going through the dressage pattern.

She learned the movements quickly. We accomplished in 2½ weeks what our class had been teaching their horses all summer, and made it to the fair – placing second in the final test. We entered a few open classes, too, and placed, even though Nell still didn't want to take her left lead. This should have been the happy ending, but it wasn't.

By late fall I stopped treating the foot. The proud flesh was reduced to a small line of scar tissue and I was going to let it finish healing that way, putting a little ointment on it now and then to keep it soft. Nell was in our big field (above the horse pasture and narrow creek bottom) with the rest of the horses, for fall and winter pasture. I was only checking on her every few days.

A few weeks after the fair I hiked up there to put more ointment on her foot, but Nell wasn't with the other horses. I finally saw her up on the ridge – outside our fence. My heart sank. She wouldn't be all by herself unless something was dreadfully wrong, and I was already guessing. I had a halter, so I put it on Ginger and rode her bareback up the steep hill, trying to keep from sliding off her rump as she lunged up the slope.

Nell was cut up again, both front feet this time. She'd taken out about 30 yards of fence in her struggles. The old posts were broken off and the whole fence had been dragged down the hill from where it originally stood. Nell had been there a long time. The blood on her front legs was dried and those legs were so swollen and stiff she could hardly move. Something must have spooked her through the fence.

She was *so* glad to see me, so forlorn and hurt. After the ordeal we'd just been through to heal her earlier wound, it broke my heart. I sent Ginger back down the hill and put the halter on Nell. I gently coaxed her across the strands of barbed wire on the ground and it took more than an hour to lead her down off the hill, one careful step at a time. Every step she took was torture. She tried so hard to move, but the pain made her tremble and she tried to carry most of her weight on her hind legs – which is very difficult while going downhill.

We finally made it down to the field and shuffled painfully across the creek. It was almost dark when I got her down to the barnyard. I treated her wounds with what I had on hand, then drove to town for more medication. As I left, she called out to me – that same unearthly lonely sound she'd made when Amahl died and when I came to get her up on that ridge. It gave me such a horribly helpless feeling to have her looking so trustingly to me for help when there was nothing more I could do to ease her pain.

Thus began another six months of doctoring, only this time it was harder because it was both front legs, and winter. For the first three weeks we didn't know if Nell would survive. She wouldn't put much weight on those legs and spent so much time lying down that we worried she might just give up or get pneumonia. A horse can't breathe very well, continually lying on its side; the lungs cannot fully fill with air. I carried feed and water to her, but most of it sat untouched as she grew thinner. She didn't seem to care.

Finally she slowly began to improve. I treated her wounds twice a day all winter. By spring she was healing nicely and I began to ride her a little every day to give her the exercise she needed to strengthen and lengthen the injured tendons and reduce the swelling in her front legs. From that point on, however, the sheath around the flexor tendon in each front leg would swell if she didn't get enough exercise.

Years flew by and Nell continued to be a great cowhorse. The scars remained on her front feet, but once she got back in shape, she was able to handle cattle work in tough terrain just like she always did. She had several more foals, two fillies and two colts. The filly she had in 1962 (Nikki) grew up to be the best cowhorse I ever had (even more agile than her mother), sired by that same little Arab stallion.

While Nikki was growing up, however, I used Nell for the difficult cattle drives and cow chasing. We had many wild adventures, including the time I was chasing a cow down through the field to bring her home. The cow dodged across a ditch to try to run back up country and I had to try to head her off. The cow crossed in a good spot, but the rest of the ditch was lined with tall rosebriars like a hedge.

Nell never hesitated from her fast gallop; she simply jumped the ditch and hedge in one huge leap, landing several feet lower on the downhill side. I wasn't expecting such a big jump and I came clear out of the saddle, losing my stirrups, but fortunately landed back in the saddle again – rather ungracefully – as she continued her mad dash to head the cow before she got to the brushy creek bottom.

Nell finally retired from hard ranch work in her mid twenties and died peacefully and suddenly, perhaps from a heart attack, a few years later. There was something special between her and me, something I never really gained to that degree with any other horse. I've had a lot of good horses over the years, but the bond of trust I had with Nell meant more – perhaps because her confidence was so hard to win. My other horses have meant a lot, too, but in different ways. The ones I raised myself, I usually had their confidence from the beginning. The bond of understanding between Nell and me – which grew out of so much heartache, tears and hard work when I was a girl, has never been equaled.

SCRAPPY
Fun to Ride

The first spring my family was on the ranch (1956, when I finished sixth grade), my dad decided to buy another horse. Ginger (the orphan filly) and Nell (the Thoroughbred filly) were young and untrained. Possum was getting old. Nosey (the big buckskin mare we won at the grocery store) was versatile and dependable, but sometimes we needed several horses to gather and round up cattle.

Dad was looking for a young horse that was already trained. Charlie Thomas (a rancher on the other side of town) had a five-year-old mare for sale. So one afternoon after school I went with Dad to the Thomas ranch to look at the mare. She was coal black, and very gentle. One of Charlie's teenage sons saddled her and rode her around the barnyard and up the hill, to demonstrate her smooth gait and maneuverability. Her name was Scrappy. She got that name as a baby because she'd been a feisty little scrapper.

Charlie bought Scrappy as a small foal, with her mother Misty for his two young sons. Lynn, the youngest son, was a year older

71

than me, and Scrappy was actually his horse – but now he was selling her, to buy sheep. The interesting sequel to this story is that 10 years later Lynn and I got married.

But back to the story of Scrappy.

Dad and I were impressed by the nice-looking black mare, her eager willingness to please her rider, and how smooth she was to ride. I'd never seen a horse that travelled like she did. Instead of trotting, Scrappy had a fast gait called a "singlefoot" or rack. Each leg moved separately in a one-two-three-four beat instead of a two-beat trot in which diagonal legs move together in unison. But unlike a four-beat walk, the singlefoot was as fast as a trot and smooth as silk – the rider never bounced.

I learned later that Scrappy's mother Misty was a pacer (a lateral gait, moving the legs on each side forward together, rather than diagonal pairs). Scrappy's singlefoot was a sort of broken pace, with the legs moving separately instead of in pairs.

Dad bought the mare and the next challenge was to get her home. She was nervous and didn't want to step up into our borrowed horse trailer the next afternoon. It took a lot of coaxing and firm persuasion. Once in the trailer, however, she didn't protest; she stood as still as a statue, trembling. By the time we got to our ranch 20 miles later, and went to unload her, I was surprised to see that Scrappy was covered with white lather. She had worried and fretted so much that she'd worked herself into a heavy sweat – and was very glad to get out of that trailer!

I led her around our barnyard until she calmed down, then let her graze while I brushed her to get off all that lather. She was nervous and fidgety; she'd grab a bite of grass then look around, whinnying. Scrappy didn't like being away from other horses.

When I put her out with our horses she was very glad to see them – though she immediately made it clear to Ginger and Nell that she was bigger and tougher than they were. They meekly kept out of her way. But Possum and Nosey didn't want to give up their leadership positions to a newcomer. After Possum chased her and bit her, Scrappy grudgingly acknowledged that he was boss. After settling their ranking, it looked like they were getting along fine.

And they did, except for one time when I'd left Possum tied to the fence when I came into the house. Mom had me hold my nine-month-old baby sister for a few minutes while she was busy doing something and suddenly I heard squealing and thudding. I looked out the window and Possum was on the ground, still tied to the fence, and Scrappy was whamming him in the belly with her hind feet!

She apparently resented the fact that Possum was boss, and decided to take advantage of him while he was tied up and couldn't defend himself. I'm not sure how he ended up on the ground but I was sure she was about to kill him! I set my baby sister on a chair and ran outside to rescue my horse, and later got thoroughly scolded for leaving the baby in a precarious spot. I figured mom could grab the baby; I had to save Possum! I chased Scrappy away and turned my attention to the old gelding, who simply lay there groaning. When I untied him, however, he rolled upright, lurched to his feet, shook himself, and took off after Scrappy to give her a piece of his mind and a feel of his teeth. She never challenged his authority again.

The new mare didn't like to be caught. She was as elusive as Nosey whenever a person approached with a halter or bridle. But when I brought the whole herd down to our corral every day after catching old Possum to ride bareback down from the Cheney Creek pasture, Scrappy loved her grain reward and was easier to catch in the small corral. I fed them oats in their individual feed boxes and then caught whichever horses were needed for the day to check or move range cattle.

Scrappy was fun to ride. We never had to urge her. It was more a matter of holding her down to a reasonable speed; her smooth single-foot gait covered the ground as swiftly as a fast-trotting horse. Her biggest fault was being too eager to get home again. She always knew which direction home was. No matter what we were doing on the range – checking gates, fences or cattle, moving cattle or searching for missing ones – Scrappy always had her mind more on going home than on the job at hand. If her rider had to head off a cow and was traveling for a brief time in the direction of home, Scrappy would try to keep going toward home rather than stopping to turn the cow. Her rider had to be firm at times, to convince her that it was not yet time to go home.

She always took the most direct route home if we were headed that direction. She'd rather go over a log or a big rock or across a bog or gully (instead of going around it) if the obstacle lay in her path. My brother and I jokingly claimed that a person could blindfold her and put her anywhere in the mountains and she would know exactly which way to go home. Her rider had to be her "brains" and guide her over the trails, or Scrappy would head straight home, even if it meant tripping over sagebrush in her way.

But everyone enjoyed riding her because she travelled so freely and willingly and had such a smooth gait. I rode her to town for 4-H meetings during the summer of 1960, as a substitute for Nell, recovering from a severe wire cut. I borrowed one of Ravndal's horses for dressage lessons since most of those movements

Lynn Thomas and Scrappy as a foal.

required trotting. But for the regular 4-H work, I used Scrappy.

Our 5-H Wranglers club held a play-day that summer, as a change from lessons and drill practice. We did games on horseback and novelty races, and a variety of team competitions and relay races. Some of the advanced riders competed in timed events like barrel races, keyhole race and pole bending if their horses were far enough along to do fast work without becoming upset and confused. As conscientious riders, we didn't push our horses into games, contests or races before they were physically and mentally ready.

We trained our horses gradually for these contests, working through the patterns slowly until they were able to handle them at speed with good control and manners. We started out at the walk, then the trot, and finally a controlled canter, before trying it as a timed event. During those practices I was wishing I could ride Nell for the play-day competitions, because she and I had progressed to the point where we were a good team; she was agile and fast and knew how to respond to my cues. I didn't even try most of the races with Scrappy because her singlefoot gait was not as fast as a gallop, and she didn't have the agility for quick stops and turns.

Instead, we participated in team contests – relays, flag race, potato race, boot race and water race. In the flag race the rider had to grab a flag (sticking out of a bucket) at the starting line, gallop to the far end of the arena and stick the flag into a second bucket, and gallop back. If the horse didn't want to get close to the bucket, the rider lost precious seconds. In the potato race, each team had an empty keg at the starting point and another keg filled with potatoes at the other end of the arena. The riders took turns using a long stick to spear a potato out of the keg at the far end and carry it back to knock the potato into the empty keg and hand the stick to the next team member.

For the boot race, all the riders put one of their boots in a pile, then lined up at the other end of the arena while one of our leaders scrambled the boots. At the starting signal, all of us raced down to the boot pile, dismounted, and tried to find our own boot, put it on, mount up and hurry back to the starting line. Scrappy and I actually came in fourth in the boot race.

But we did best in the water race. Each rider had to dip a full glass of water from a barrel at the starting point and hurry to the other end of the arena to place it on top of a second barrel. The rider who got to the other end with the most water was the winner. It's difficult to hold a glass of water level when your horse is trotting or galloping, but Scrappy's gait was so smooth we didn't spill a drop.

Our team also won the dipper race. Each team had a rider holding an empty bucket and another rider at the other end of the arena holding a full bucket. The teams chose their members with the calmest and steadiest horses as bucket holders. At the starting signal, each team sent a rider carrying a dipper to the far end to get water out of the full bucket and bring the dipper back to be emptied into their team's bucket. The team who had the most water in that bucket when they got finished was the winner. It was nice to be speedy, but even more important to not spill the water!

We had fun at the playday, then it was back to lessons, getting ready for our 4-H horse show – a couple weeks ahead of the Fair. We also practiced our mounted drill for the fair. I wanted to ride Nell at the fair in our 4-H dressage test and the rodeo queen contest, but I used Scrappy in horse show because Nell wasn't quite recovered enough.

My friend Marilyn Muench and I decided to dress up as knights for the costume class. We used bright green horse blankets – borrowed from Ravndals – that looked like the fancy cloth worn by the chargers in the Middle Ages. Marilyn's mom gave us some old bed sheets to make our costumes. We sewed matching tops and dyed them bright yellow. On the front we sewed a dragon emblem that I painted on lightweight cardboard. From another sheet we created long capes and dyed them bright red, to wear over our shoulders. We made helmets out of tin foil and cardboard, with a cloth draped over the back – just like we'd seen in pictures. Marilyn's little brother had toy swords and shields, so we borrowed those. Colorful tights and cardboard sandals completed our outfits, along with some fringed cloth we sewed onto our bridle reins.

That was the only summer I rode Scrappy in 4-H, as a substitute for Nell. But in 1959, I raised a foal from Scrappy for a mare and foal project. I had always wanted to raise a foal, and my parents consented to let me use Scrappy. I rode her down to the Ravndal's ranch in May of 1958 and left her there for a week to be bred to their Arabian stallion El Khamis.

The foal was due about April 20 the next spring. I was eager for that baby to arrive, but I was also worried because we didn't have a very good place for Scrappy to foal. I decided to put her in the round corral in the barnyard, so I cleaned that corral, picked up several old poles, and made sure there were no nails sticking out of the fence.

My family was still living in town during winters. My Dad had a hired couple at the ranch looking after the cattle and feeding the cows. I talked my parents into letting me stay with the hired couple while I waited for Scrappy to foal, because I wanted to be there when the baby arrived. I slept in a sleeping bag in the upstairs of the old ranch house where the hired couple was staying. On school days I rode Ginger the four miles to the highway to catch the school bus, leaving her in Lester Withington's corral for the day and riding her back to the ranch after school.

As Scrappy's belly got bigger, I kept checking her udder to see if it was filling with milk. A couple weeks before she was due to foal, I put her in the round corral, separate from the other horses, and started checking on her during the nights. This would be Scrappy's first foal, and I didn't want anything to go wrong.

She was confined in the corral, so I exercised her daily after school, leading or riding her. I watered her every morning and evening since there was no water in that corral. We didn't have much hay left, and most of it was moldy, so I diligently sorted out the best parts of the bales for her. Scrappy was thin, except for her big belly. The hired man didn't think mares needed grain, and

Scrappy

Heidi and Scrappy.

thought horses could get by just fine on the "leftover" hay from the cows. I practically had to fight for every flake of good hay I fed Scrappy. He then fed the milk cow's calf the last of the good hay and left the moldy hay for my mare. I was very worried about her and bought some grain to feed her.

Scrappy's belly got bigger and bigger and her udder fuller, but still no foal. Her due date came and went, and Scrappy still hadn't foaled. My school work suffered, those weeks I stayed at the ranch, because there wasn't much time for homework. I got up at 5 a.m. to feed and water Scrappy and get to the school bus on time, riding Ginger, and went to bed at 8 a.m. since I was getting up in the middle of the night to check on Scrappy.

The weather was mostly nice, but one morning there was seven inches of new snow. Ginger and I got down to the Withington ranch on time to catch the bus in spite of the slippery mud under all that snow. Scrappy went a week past her due date, and Ravndals drove up to the ranch to check on her. They gave her an injection of vitamin A and D, since our hay was so poor quality. The first of May came and went. Scrappy was long overdue. I hadn't expected it to take this long!

One evening she seemed more restless than usual and I noticed a whitish ooze on the ends of her teats. Mrs. Ravndal had told me that most mares "wax" within about 24 hours of foaling. This is the plug working out of the teat, in readiness for milk flow.

That night I crept quietly downstairs with my flashlight and put my boots on outside. I was always very careful to not wake the hired man and his wife when I got up at night to check on Scrappy. A chill wind was blowing, and a light sprinkling of snow covered the ground. The moonlight made the barnyard bright and I didn't need my flashlight. As I approached the larger corral by the cow barn I saw Scrappy, standing at the gate, wanting to come out. I don't know how she got out of the round corral. She may have unhooked the horseshoe latch, maybe nudging it with her nose, and then pushed against the big pole gate into the larger pen.

She whinnied softly as I approached. She hadn't foaled yet, so I put a rope around her neck and led her back to the round corral. She stood by the gate and whinnied as I left and made my way back to the house.

When I went back out to the corral at 5 a.m. (May 5th) there was three inches of fresh snow. As I approached the corral I stopped and stared. Not one, but two dark forms awaited me in the dim light. The little foal was wet, cold and shivering. I could hardly believe my eyes; Scrappy had been so long overdue that it took a moment to acknowledge the miracle in front of me. I hurried into

Scrappy in 1960 with a sod-roofed shed in the background.

the corral to check Scrappy's udder to see if the foal – a little bay filly – had nursed.

She had already nursed and seemed fine. Scrappy was a good mother and jealously protected her baby from me. I had to speak firmly to her because she didn't want me handling her baby. I ran back to the house to get the bottle of iodine, and when I came back to the corral, Scrappy made a fuss when I tied her up so I could handle the foal. The wet little rascal was quite a handful as I cornered her by the fence next to Scrappy, but I got the navel stump thoroughly dipped into the iodine.

The filly was bay, like her sire, with black mane and tail, black legs, and had a white star in her forehead. Scrappy fretted and pawed the ground until I turned her loose again. Then she nickered at her baby and nuzzled her all over to make sure she was okay – and hurried off to the far side of the corral with the baby following right behind her. It was a pretty sight, with the filly lifting her dainty little legs high in the air as she pranced through the snow with her head up and her little tail straight in the air. My heart lurched with joy to watch them – the black mare doing her smooth singlefoot and the baby trotting along behind. The baby inherited her Arabian sire's gaits as well as coloring.

By the time I got back to the house to get ready for school, there was no time to eat breakfast, and I was almost too late to catch the school bus. There was not enough time to catch and saddle Ginger so I just sprinted down the snowy road. My feet flew as I ran and jogged the three miles to the Withington Ranch. It was a beautiful day with sunshine sparkling on the new-fallen snow, and it was the most wonderful day in the world because I now had a new baby filly!

Scrappy raised a nice foal, and in later years we tried to breed her again, but without success. She spent the rest of her career at our place as a ranch horse, and as an occasional mount for guests because she was so easy to ride. My city cousins loved her because they didn't have to endure a trot and could keep up with me in comfort when I took them range riding.

My dad rode her to get our Christmas tree one cold December day, up on our 320-acre pasture, and pulled it behind her through the snow. She sweated, climbing up there, and I vividly remember him coming home dragging the tree, with Scrappy covered in frost, looking like a white horse instead of a black one. The humorous part was that we had a visit from the game warden the next day. He'd seen the drag trail, and came to see if we'd poached a deer and dragged it home!

KHAMETTE
My First Foal

S crappy foaled in the early morning of May 5th, 1959, in several inches of new snow. I was so excited, telling all my friends at school about the new filly. I seemed to float through the day, my mind far from my school work; I couldn't wait to get back to the ranch and see my baby. During the noon hour I phoned my parents, and my 4-H leaders Jerry and Velma Ravndal, to give them the wonderful news. I named the baby Khamette, after her sire El Khamis. It was pronounced like comet, except the accent would be on the second syllable.

By late afternoon the snow had melted and the new grass was greener than ever. The whole countryside had a brighter look as I rode the bus home, partly because I was so happy. When I got off the bus I sprinted and jogged the three miles back up to the ranch.

My 4-H leaders drove to our place to see the new foal, arriving about the same time I did. My parents came shortly after, eager to see the filly. She was beautiful! But one alarming note sent a stab of worry into my heart. Her long slim legs looked different than they had that morning. All four pasterns and fetlock joints were puffy and swollen, and on her hind legs the swelling was nearly up to her hocks. The Ravndals told me this was probably navel ill or joint ill, which is actually septicemia.

The unusual thing was that it had appeared so quickly; usually the infection enters at the raw, moist navel stump soon after birth and then travels through the blood stream and may settle into the joints and/or internal organs. It usually takes a day or two for the legs to become swollen. This foal was born with the infection already circulating through her system. Ravndals drove back to town to talk to the veterinarian and Dad went to town to buy penicillin so we could start treating the filly.

The probable explanation for the infection was that Scrappy had a low-grade uterine infection and the filly picked it up shortly before or during birth. Dad had tried to raise a foal from Scrappy a couple years earlier, and had sent her to a ranch near Challis, Idaho, to be bred. That rancher was of the "old school" thinking that a maiden mare should be "opened up" to remove constricting tissues in the vagina before she is bred. He may have used unsanitary tools to do this. Scrappy did not settle to that breeding.

We found out later that Scrappy did have a reproductive tract infection, and we were very lucky that she became pregnant when bred to El Khamis, and that she was able to carry the foal to term. This was the only foal she could have. The next couple of years we tried again to breed her, but with no luck.

Our challenge at the moment, however, was to save this filly from being crippled with joint infection. We gave her a large dose of penicillin (10 cc) the first evening, and 5 cc daily thereafter, for a week. The swelling in her legs diminished markedly by the second day and was completely gone by the end of the week.

Scrappy and baby lived in the small pen by the barnyard while we were treating the foal. After we were sure Khamette's infection was cleared up, we put them up Cheney Creek with the other horses because we were out of hay. When I led Scrappy through the corral (with foal following close at her side) and turned them out, the other horses came galloping down to inspect the baby. The filly was also curious about them and sniffed noses with Ginger – making chewing motions with her mouth.

I'd seen other foals do this "chewing" when meeting or greeting adult horses, and wondered why they did that. Jerry Ravndal said he wasn't sure, but maybe they did it as a way of telling the big horses, "I'm just little. Please don't hurt me!"

But Scrappy didn't want any of them getting that close to her baby. She put her ears back and ran at the other mares to try to bite them, then swiftly whirled and lashed out with her hind feet. Ginger and Nell quickly got the message and ran off. Even Nosey and Old Possum (who ordinarily bossed Scrappy around) decided that this aggressively protective mama was nothing to mess with.

After that, Scrappy and her baby were accepted as part of the herd, though Scrappy tried to keep Khamette close by her side as they grazed. She stayed between the filly and the other horses, gently herding her away if any of the others came too close. The filly learned about climbing hills, jumping gullies and logs, and finding the best trails through the brush and trees along the creek.

I helped my father on weekends, fixing fences, and we built a new section of fence so that when school was out we'd have a small pasture next to the orchard and garden, for Scrappy and her foal. Then I wouldn't have to hike up Cheney Creek every day to find them. We also created a large "stall" between our sod-roofed sheds. This would be a place to work with the mare and foal in the mornings or evenings when I wasn't riding range, irrigating, or riding Nell to town for our 4-H meetings.

On June 8 I brought the horses down from the hills. Khamette was shy because she hadn't seen people for three weeks, and Scrappy was skittish, not wanting anyone to get close to her baby. My dad helped me corner them at one end of the corral so I could quietly slip closer and put a halter on Scrappy. Then I led her, with baby following, to the new little pasture.

Khamette was a month old by then and hadn't been handled since that first week when we gave her all those penicillin shots. She was sassy and elusive, not wanting to be caught. I worked with her several times each day, putting her and Scrappy in the stall between the sheds where it was easier to patiently corner and catch the foal. This was a perfect place to catch her, and a safe place to leave her if I needed to ride Scrappy.

Every morning I caught Scrappy with a little grain for a reward, and led her to the pen between the sheds, with Khamette trotting along behind. Then I could tie Scrappy to the pole fence and shut the gate behind them. That was the beginning of many daily sessions of patient work to gentle the filly. At first she was shy about being touched and hid behind Scrappy or ducked under her neck to get away from me. I took my time and didn't even try to catch her, the first couple days. I just sat on the pole fence talking to her and Scrappy, getting the filly used to my voice.

After Khamette began to accept my presence and relax, not trying to dash away from me, I began tying Scrappy during these sessions because she always tried to stay between me and her baby. I

Khamette

Khamette at two months old, during an early leading lesson.

spent a lot of time brushing Scrappy, picking up her feet and cleaning them, letting Khamette realize that having a human around was normal, and that Scrappy trusted and accepted me. Before long, Khamette's sassy curiosity overcame her fears and she came to sniff me. I might be bent over, cleaning one of Scrappy's feet, and feel the filly's moist breath or a little nibble at the back of my shirt.

Eventually she grew bolder and I could reach out my hand and touch her. After that, I could quietly corner her between the tied mare and the fence or the shed wall. At first I didn't try to put a halter on the baby. I held her with one arm around her front and one around her hindquarters, letting the filly realize she couldn't get away. After a few times of being gently restrained by my arms, Khamette quit trying to struggle, and she'd stand there as I scratched and petted her. I started touching her all over, so she'd get used to the feel of my hands and not be startled. Soon she seemed to enjoy this attention and didn't fidget or try to get away.

As she got used to me, and bolder, she became sassier – and sometimes tried to nip or kick. I had to prevent these naughty actions and teach her to behave nicely. She had to learn not only to trust me (and not be afraid) but also to respect me. After several days, she no longer tried to kick when I ran my hands down her legs and under her belly.

She soon came up to me to be caught rather than trying to run away. I fed Scrappy grain every day, and Khamette would nibble some. By this time I was able to put a rope around her neck and nose in a sort of halter. Then my dad had Clyde Stone (at the saddle shop) make a tiny foal halter/hackamore.

I could quietly corner Khamette, hold her with one arm, and slip the halter on her. The first time I tried to lead her, however, she stubbornly pulled back. I had to use another rope to loop around the filly's rump. Then when Khamette pulled back, I could give a little pull on the rump rope to encourage her to move forward again. Then I was able to lead her all around the small pen. The filly was beginning to trust me more, and not fight. It was a little harder when I led her out of the little pen and away from her mother. The hardest part was coming back to mama; she wanted to run, and was quite a handful to hold back to a prancing trot. Scrappy was not happy about being tied while her baby was led away. She whinnied and pawed the ground and it took awhile before she settled down and became more patient while I worked with the filly.

Eventually I was able to lead her in small circles in the barnyard, and gradually took Khamette farther away from her mama. She was almost two months old by then, and a lot bigger and stronger than when she was a baby. There was one time I couldn't hold her. I'd led Khamette to the top of our lane where it joined the county road. A covey of quail flew up and startled the filly. She whirled around and took off at a dead run, heading back to mama. She got up so much speed so quickly that I couldn't stop her, or keep up with her, and lost my footing. As I tripped and fell, it spooked the filly even more, and she put on a fresh burst of speed.

I had fallen to my knees and couldn't continue hanging onto the rope without dragging along the ground on my stomach. I had to let go, hoping and praying that the scared foal wouldn't run into a fence. But she ran straight back to the barnyard and into the pen where Scrappy was tied — and I came running and puffing after her.

After she calmed down I led her back out again. I didn't want to end the lesson on that bad note; I didn't want Khamette to try to pull away from me again, thinking she could run back to mama whenever she wanted. I led her around until she quit prancing and was calm and relaxed, walking nicely beside me.

During each lesson I picked up Khamette's feet, teaching her to shift her weight. At first she didn't know how to balance herself and tried to take her foot away, and nearly fell down. So when I picked up a foot I'd lean against her to steady her and force her weight onto the other legs. She soon learned to shift her weight herself whenever I gently squeezed the back of her fetlock joint or tickled the back of her pastern to encourage her to pick up that foot. I wanted her to be very nice about having her feet handled, so that she would be easy to trim and shoe. I wanted to be able to shoe Khamette myself. I practiced cleaning her little feet each day with a hoof pick, and tapping on them to get her used to what would happen later. When her little feet started to grow long, I carefully trimmed and smoothed them with the rasp so they wouldn't chip.

Next came tying lessons. I started tying Khamette to the sturdy pole fence, next to her mother. The first time I tied her, she pulled back, and I had to push on her rump to push her forward again so she wouldn't hurt her neck muscles. After finding that she couldn't get away, Khamette resigned herself to being tied up. After a few lessons she'd stand patiently. I didn't leave her tied for very long at a time, however, because at that young age she became bored quickly.

It was easy to teach her to lead at the trot, on cue, and to stop on command. To encourage her to trot, I merely moved my own feet faster, jogging in place, while telling her to "trot!" in a crisp tone of voice. She soon realized this was the signal to move faster, and we'd trot up and down the lane together, with her shoulder right beside me. Before long, Khamette associated voice commands with the proper actions and would walk, trot or halt just on spoken command.

I was very proud of her accomplishments. Khamette led so easily and naturally that I often trotted her in circles, figure eights, in and out through a line of posts (that my brother and I had set in the ground for a fence around our garden) and various other patterns, to test her maneuverability. I did more ground work with this filly than any other horse I raised, partly because she was my first and I wanted her to learn everything I could possibly teach her, and partly because at that stage of my life (15 years old) I had time to do it. I tied a saddle blanket on her back and led her around. She quickly became accustomed to whatever I tried with her. By then, she and Scrappy were up Cheney Creek again with the other horses, and whenever I hiked up there in the mornings to bring them down, Khamette was always the first to come running up to me.

Khamette, at three months old, taking a nap in the pasture.

Summer passed quickly, and it was almost time for the Fair. Since Scrappy and Khamette were my mare and foal project, I'd kept detailed records on everything I did with them. I would also show them in the mare and foal class. I wanted Khamette to be well trained and well mannered.

The fairgrounds had several rows of box stalls and tie stalls, and I wanted to take my mare and foal a day before the horse classes, to be sure of having a box stall – since I would have to leave Scrappy and Khamette there a couple of days. My dad brought a bale of hay in our jeep, a small sack of grain, and my feed tub and water bucket.

We didn't have a horse trailer, so I planned to ride Scrappy and lead Khamette the 14 miles to town. Khamette had outgrown her baby halter by then, so I bought a fancy foal halter, with a long lead rope. I also had a leather lead shank that I planned to use when showing the filly. I practiced riding Scrappy around the barnyard and leading Khamette, and she led very nicely alongside her mama.

Early that morning we started our trip. I rode Scrappy and led four-month-old Khamette alongside. She trotted to keep up with Scrappy's swift singlefoot as we headed down the dirt road. By the time we reached the highway we'd already met one car, and Khamette had been a little frightened, but stayed close to Scrappy as the car went by, reassured by the mare's calm attitude. Along the highway, I rode down the borrow-pit, as far away from the pavement as possible. Passing vehicles didn't scare the mare and foal after we'd met a few. The filly kept up with Scrappy and didn't get tired. We made the trip in three hours and headed into the fairgrounds.

Scrappy whinnied nervously and Khamette was wide-eyed with curiosity, looking at all the strange horses. I found the stall where my father had left my buckets and hay and got the two horses settled in. Scrappy nibbled at hay, but spent most of her time looking out the open top door, watching all the activity. Khamette was almost too short, but by stretching her neck she was able to watch, too.

My mom, dad and brother drove to the Fairgrounds later that day to look at the exhibits. I went back home to the ranch with my family so Rocky and I could ride Ginger and Nell to town that afternoon, to be ready for the 4-H classes and regular horse classes the next morning. This was the first time that we and our horses had ever stayed overnight at the fairgrounds, and we thought it would be fun, sleeping in sleeping bags next to our horses' stalls.

I was nervous and excited the next morning, and glad the

Khamette – an early tying lesson.

riding classes came first because these were something I'd done before. My brother and I both placed in the top third of our class, to get blue ribbons, and rode back to the barn to put our horses away and get Khamette and Scrappy ready for the mare and foal class. I'd hung Khamette's new halter and leather lead strap on a nail, high on the wall – out of the foal's reach, or so I thought. Somehow Khamette had pulled it down and chewed the leather strap, making it all wrinkled and tattered. I smoothed it as best I could, but it still looked crumpled. Rocky helped me lead them out of the stall and down to the arena, where the mare and foal class was about to begin. Scrappy was nervous and snorting, and Rocky had his hands full keeping her down to a prancing walk, while I led the skittish foal alongside.

In spite of being nervous and excited with all the other horses nearby, they behaved reasonably well and I was able to show what

Khamette and I had accomplished in our summer of lessons. When it was our turn to perform, Rocky held Scrappy and I led Khamette away from her, leading her up and down the arena at the walk, then a trot, and bringing her to quick stop – to let her stand for a moment before backing up, picking up her feet, and then leading her in a big circle in both directions. Then I led her back to her impatient mother who was whinnying and pawing the ground.

I was delighted to receive a blue ribbon for my mare and foal project, but totally surprised to receive the overall 4-H trophy for best project – based on my detailed record-books, scrapbook and performance in the classes. The trophy was a beautiful bronze mare and foal, standing on a wooden plaque.

After the Fair was over, we took the horses home. I rode Scrappy and led Khamette, and Rocky rode Ginger and led Nell. It had been a very exciting and tiring three days! I was glad Khamette's little black feet were hard and tough. Even after traveling the 14 miles, twice, she was not sorefooted.

School started a few days later and I didn't have time to work with the horses. I turned Scrappy and Khamette out in the Cheney Creek pasture until it was time to wean the filly later that fall. After weaning, I let Scrappy go back up Cheney Creek with the other horses. The filly didn't whinny for her anymore. Instead, she looked forward to my coming to feed and brush her every day after school. She remembered all her lessons and good manners, and I was looking forward to when she'd be old enough to ride. It had been a great learning experience for me, raising her from a baby and doing all her training myself.

KHAMETTE GROWS UP
Learning Together

After she was weaned, Khamette spent the winter with a group of heifer calves in the big corral. The creek ran through it, so Khamette and the calves had water; I didn't have to carry water to the filly – like when she was in the round corral being weaned. When it got cold, however, the creek froze over, and we had to chop holes in the ice.

The replacement heifers were good company for Khamette and she wasn't lonely. The other horses did fine up Cheney Creek, pawing through snow to get to grass. But a weanling needs more protein than dry grass, so I kept her in the corral where she'd get good hay with the heifers, and I could feed her grain. It was also good experience for Khamette because she grew up being totally at ease with cattle.

School kept me busy, but I worked with my filly whenever I could, tying her, brushing her, cleaning her feet, leading her on long walks. A person can teach a horse many things before riding, which makes training easier when the horse is old enough to ride.

This would be a busy year working with my horses, along with helping Dad with range riding, fence-fixing, haying and irrigating. I planned to use Nell again as my 4-H riding project, doing some advanced jumping and dressage. I also had a horseshoeing project. I wanted to learn more about shoeing, and corrective trimming.

Khamette's front legs were not perfect and I needed to keep her feet trimmed properly so those legs wouldn't grow crooked. Her cannon bones were offset to the outside rather than centered below the knees, which put her feet too far apart. Her hoofs were also a bit crooked. Instead of pointing straight forward, her toes pointed slightly inward (pigeon toed). Thus her legs didn't move forward in a straight line when she walked; instead, they paddled outward. Since they landed crooked and were picked up to the outside of the toe instead of straight, she wore her feet unevenly. Unless they were frequently trimmed to keep them more symmetrical, they would become even more crooked as she grew, because of the uneven way they were wearing.

My 4-H leader Jerry Ravndal was an excellent farrier and gave me lots of good advice, showing me how to trim Khamette's front feet to keep them well balanced and traveling straighter. He also showed me the proper way to use shoeing tools, and loaned me books on horseshoeing.

That winter I did a lot of studying. Our 4-H group was also studying various aspects of horsemanship and horse training, learning more about conformation and soundness, and taking written tests. When spring came, we met at the Fairgrounds with our horses, and I rode Nell to the practice sessions as often as I could, but I was helping Dad a lot with the ranch that summer –

especially the irrigating. It was a very dry year and we needed to keep the hayfields green and growing with water from the creek. I usually rode Ginger to irrigate, and looked forward to when Khamette would be big enough to ride and use for this job.

This year, however, I was hoping to show her in the Fair in a halter class, and in our 4-H yearling class. As soon as the grass was growing enough, I put Khamette in the small pasture by the house. One morning when I went out to catch her, I discovered that she'd been too curious about a porcupine. Her muzzle was covered with quills! They were stuck deeply into her upper and lower lip and every time she tried to eat grass, she bumped the quills and poked them deeper into the flesh.

She liked to play with our cats and dog, and maybe she thought she could play with a porcupine. I put her halter on, careful to not bump any of the quills. Then I tried to pull them out – but that caused more pain. Khamette was so nervous and upset by the time I'd pulled out three quills that I realized I needed help.

There were at least 30 quills stuck into the filly's muzzle. Rocky and I tried to keep her calm while Dad pulled out the quills with pliers. She jumped around a little, so my brother held her halter and I picked up a front foot and held it firmly – so she couldn't move around so much. Each time Dad grasped some quills with pliers (usually two or three at once because they were jammed into her nose so thickly), he pulled them out with a quick movement before she could pull away. She'd always try to pull back, but then I'd talk to her and get her calm again. Eventually she realized we were trying to help, and stood there trembling on three legs, shaking her head a little. Dad was able to get all the quills out and I checked the inside of her mouth, to make sure there were none broken off inside her lip. I comforted and petted her, then rubbed the bloody spots off her nose – which seemed to make the stinging pain go away. I fed her a little grain as a reward for being such a good girl.

I'd sold an article about our 5-H club to *Farm Journal* and that spring they sent a photographer to take pictures. Khamette and I were on the cover. When school was out for the summer, I had more time to work with the filly. She already knew how to lead at the walk and trot, with me moving alongside her left shoulder, holding the halter rope a few inches from the halter, and the rest of the rope looped (not coiled) safely in my other hand. I'd learned that you never hold a lead rope in coils that could encircle your hand or wrist if the horse bolted and got away. It's safer to keep it in neat loops so that you can play out more rope as needed, without your hand getting caught in a circle of rope.

Now I wanted to teach her to walk, trot, and halt on voice commands, to work on a longe line (traveling in a big circle around me) and stand squarely for judging in a halter class at the Fair. It only took a few practice sessions to show Khamette what she was supposed to do. If she was standing crooked on one leg, I gently tapped or tickled that leg with a long willow stick until she moved it back into proper position. She also learned voice commands and I could lead her up and down our lane at the walk or trot, and bring her to an instant halt just by saying "whoa."

Teaching her to longe was a little more challenging because she didn't understand at first that I wanted her to travel around me in a big circle. She kept wanting to come to me, instead. I

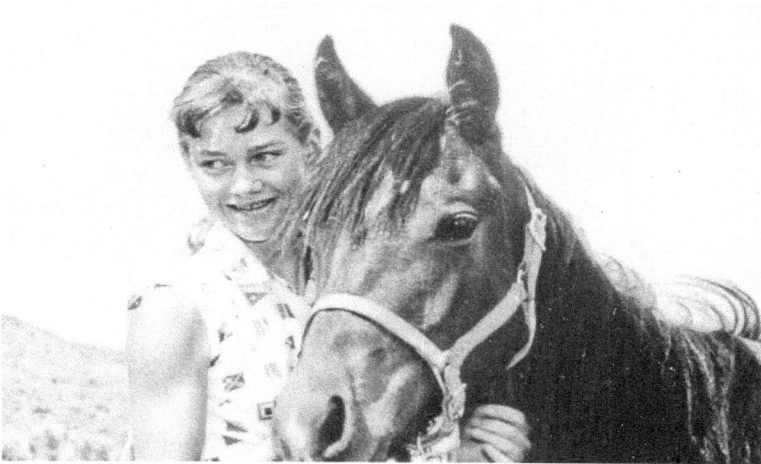

Khamette and me in 1960, when she was a yearling.

had to find a long willow (since I didn't have a longeing whip) to encourage her to stay out in the circle. At first I had to tap her gently on the rump, and use voice commands to encourage her to keep moving instead of stopping or coming to me. Once she got the idea, it was easy.

I also taught her to ground tie. This meant being able to leave her halter rope (or later the bridle reins, after she was grown up and being ridden) hanging down on the ground, and the horse standing there and not moving. I started by telling her "whoa" on the longe line, and having her stand awhile. If she started to move, I reminded her that she was supposed to stand still, with a slight tug on the line and the word "whoa" again. Soon she would obey just the voice command without any tug on the halter.

Then I started leaving her standing there with the long line on the ground, and walking a short distance away from her. If

Khamette tried to move, or to follow me, I would tell her "whoa" again and she would stand still. This lesson paid off later after I was riding her to ride range and chase cows. There were times I had to get off and walk through thick brush to get the cattle, or get a calf back through a fence (sometimes the little calves could crawl through the wires). I could get off Khamette and go into the brush or through the fence, leaving Khamette standing there waiting for me, and I'd know that she would wait patiently for my return. She trusted me and I trusted her. She never wandered off or headed for home.

When it came time for the Fair and 4-H judging I rode Nell to town and led Khamette. In the open horse show I showed Khamette in the yearling class. She only placed 4th because of her slightly crooked front legs, but in the 4-H class – where she was judged on training and manners as well as conformation, she placed second.

After the fair, and with school starting, I turned Khamette out to pasture up Cheney Creek with the other horses, and hiked up there every few days to check on her. But one day when I hiked up to see the horses, they were gone. I couldn't find them anywhere. When I hiked to the ridge at the top of the pasture I got a better view, and discovered that the top gate had been left open – maybe by deer hunters. The horses had found the open gate and had gone to the range. I found their tracks going through the gate, and followed the tracks in the snow. I hiked several miles and finally found the horses high up in the Cheney Creek canyon. I caught Ginger and rode her bareback down to the ranch, calling the others.

By March, Khamette was a little thin. The snow was deeper

and it was harder for the horses to find grass. I brought her and Nell down to the small pasture to feed them hay and grain and start working with Khamette again. I wanted to make sure the growing filly had enough food, and wanted to feed Nell better also, because she was going to have a foal later that spring.

That summer, as a two-year-old, Khamette's training continued, in preparation for when I could start riding her. I put a saddle pad on her back, and then my saddle. After a few days of saddling and unsaddling, I started leading her around with the saddle on. The first time I led her at the trot and the stirrups flopped against her, she was worried, but soon calmed down when she realized it wasn't hurting her. Then I longed her with the saddle on, at the walk and trot.

Then it was time to try a bridle. I didn't have a snaffle bit so Ravndals loaned me one of their training snaffles, and Rocky and I made a headstall from some of the old harness leather in the shed. The harness had buckles and snaps, and some pieces of good leather – after we cleaned it up. We cut some leather the proper length, and using a leather punch, rivets and buckles, we made a nice headstall. I had Khamette wear the headstall and bit when I led her or longed her, and she soon became accustomed to the feel of it, no longer trying to spit out the bit or get her tongue over it.

Next, Rocky and I improvised a bitting harness, to get her used to bit pressure. We used more harness leather to make the side reins. The end hooked to the bit, we made from a slice of old rubber tire inner tubing, so it would be stretchy. The leather part could be hooked to the cinch ring on my saddle. We also made an overcheck out of old curtain cord, running down each side of the headstall to the bit. The upper part ran from the top of the headstall back to the saddle horn. When wearing this bitting harness, Khamette could hold her head in proper position, but the overcheck would keep her from lowering her head down toward the ground, and she couldn't root her nose out too far (trying to pull on the bit) or the elastic side reins would pull her head back into place.

This helped her get used to pressure from the bit (when she pulled on it) but gave her instant relief from pressure when she "gave" to the bit, and was very easy on her mouth. The elastic rubber reins were "user friendly" but gently pulled her head back where it should be. Soon she stopped trying to pull on it and found it was much easier to "give" to the bit. This was the start of learning how to respond to a pull on the reins, and she learned this important lesson before she ever had a rider. I wanted to do a good job of training Khamette, and not ruin her mouth like the horse breaker did to Nell. I wanted Khamette to trust and respect me, and never fight or buck.

Next, I made long reins from the old harness lines and taught Khamette to drive in long lines. I hooked the long reins to the bit and put them through the stirrup bows of the saddle, so they wouldn't dangle down onto the ground where she might get a foot over them. At first she didn't understand that she was supposed to go forward with me walking behind her. She wanted to turn around and come toward me. So Rocky led her until Khamette got the idea about what she was supposed to do.

By the fifth lesson, Khamette was doing so well that I took her out in the small pasture by the orchard and we travelled

Khamette as a two-year-old in training

around the pasture. It was fun! Khamette seemed to enjoy the lessons and I thought it would be really neat to someday teach her to pull a cart. I let Rocky drive her in long lines so I could take photos of her.

We never did pull a cart, but I later used her to pull bundles of wood posts – with a lariat tied to my saddle horn – over a hill where we couldn't drive our jeep, to rebuild part of the Cheney Creek fence. I also used her to pull our Volkswagen out of a mud-hole when it got stuck. When she was 13 she pulled a water trough (with my two little kids in it) to install at a spring on the range, that we couldn't quite get to with the jeep.

By late summer two-year-old Khamette was doing so well I realized there wasn't much more I could teach her from the ground. It was time to start riding her. I kept the halter on, under the bridle, and tied the halter rope to the saddle horn, giving

Khamette enough slack to move her head and neck normally, but not enough that she could get her head down low enough to buck.

I led her to our old round corral (the one early ranchers on our creek used when running horses in off the range and breaking them), to ride her for the first time so she wouldn't be able to get up much speed if she became frightened. I put weight in the stirrup a few times, and that didn't bother her, so I got on, being careful not to startle her by bumping her. She stood quietly, and it didn't bother her at all when I shifted my weight in the saddle.

I got off and on a few times. The next day I got on her again, and asked her to move out by squeezing with my legs, but she wasn't sure what to do and stayed rooted to the ground. I tried kicking a little but she still didn't understand; she just put her ears back – telling me she didn't like it. I had to pull her head around to one side and get her off balance a little so she would take a step. Then she realized she could walk around with me on her back. All the groundwork paid off because she already knew how to turn, and stop. A few rides around the corral, and we were ready to go out into the big wide world. I rode her on short rides that fall around the pasture and up the driveway, before turning her out with the other horses to winter pasture.

I started riding her again the spring of 1962, when she was a three-year-old and I was graduating from high school. She did everything nicely, picking up where we'd left off. She was always eager to go, especially on the way home, and I didn't want to pull hard on her mouth. So I attached side reins to the halter and rode with four reins (snaffle reins and halter reins). I could hold her back with the halter as well as the bit, and not be so hard on her mouth.

Khamette had very tough feet, and I rode her for two months before she needed shoes. Jerry Ravndal helped me put the first shoes on her, and she was very well mannered. I reset those shoes myself, seven weeks later, when her feet needed trimming, and shod her myself the rest of her life.

By mid-summer I was riding range on her and she was learning about herding cows and starting to neck rein. It was time to transition from the snaffle to a curb bit. Velma Ravndal helped me select a Hartwell Pelham from a mail order catalog, and it turned out to be an excellent bit for gradually changing Khamette from snaffle to curb. I rode her a few times with just snaffle reins to get her used to the new bit, then used four reins, using the curb reins more and the snaffle reins less, and within a month we were completely transitioned to just the curb. I used that bit the rest of her life and eventually bought several more for my other horses because they worked so well.

In all her early training she never tried to buck, except once, and I don't think she meant to lose me. I'd already ridden her a lot that summer, and she was doing so well that perhaps I was overconfident, riding her like she was a well-trained reliable horse and forgetting she was still a green filly. That day, when I went to the pasture to catch Khamette for our daily ride, she had been frolicking with Nell and baby Nikki. They'd been running and bucking and having great fun.

I called Khamette and she stopped running with the mare and foal and came trotting to meet me. I saddled her and rode up through our ranch to check some gates, and was coming home down along the creek. As we rounded the bend in the "narrows" and started down the trail toward the lower pasture, Khamette suddenly bucked. I wasn't expecting it, and sailed over her head. I yelled her name as she galloped down the trail toward the creek crossing. She stopped abruptly and turned around with a confused look, as if to say, "Why are you sitting there on the ground?" She came trotting to me, and I got on again and we continued home. I think she simply forgot I was riding her, and bucked in high spirits as we came around the corner toward home, suddenly remembering the interrupted games she and the mare and foal had been playing just before our ride. She never again tried to buck with a rider.

We did a lot of range riding that summer and Khamette learned how to cross streams, jump over logs and gullies, and handle herself with good balance on steep hillsides. I helped Dad bring home one of our bulls to doctor for pinkeye, and that was a challenge because the bull didn't want to come home. Dad had to pop him on the nose a few times with his bullwhip to change his mind about trying to run back. When we got him over the hill and closer to the gate, I galloped ahead to open the gate. Khamette was becoming a useful ranch horse. She and I helped round up cattle in the fall just before I went to college. She was an eager traveler and fun to ride.

After I went to college, she encountered a rattlesnake in her pasture and was bitten on the front leg. Dad noticed she was lame. Her leg was hot and swollen, with two fang marks. He cleaned it up and gave her antibiotics. She was never ill, and the swelling went down in a few days. But from then on she was afraid of rattlesnakes. Our other horses never worried about them, but whenever Khamette heard one rattling she'd jump away from the sound.

Khamette and me riding sidesaddle, ready for the parade.

The summer of 1963, she was a four-year-old, and we traveled many miles together after I got home from college. She was my favorite horse for checking cows because she had such a fast walk and trot, always eager to go. We could cover the whole range in a lot less time than on a lazy horse that needed continual urging. The more we did together, the more we understood one another and we became a good team. This was my last year of 4-H and I had several different projects – horseshoeing, 4-H judging, and a yearling project (Nell's filly). Khamette was my four-year-old under saddle project (a continuation of my mare and foal project, yearling project and green horse project). One of the new things

107

we did together that summer was learn to ride sidesaddle – on an old borrowed sidesaddle. That was a lot different from riding a western saddle or the English flat saddle that I borrowed for jumping and dressage when I had Nell as my project.

When riding sidesaddle, the rider has all the weight on the right thigh, with only one stirrup – and the right leg curled around over the upper horn. I had to learn to post by rising up on just one leg instead of two. Most difficult, however, was not having a leg down against the right side of the horse. Khamette was so well trained to respond to leg pressure that I felt handicapped not being able to give leg signals on that side. Ladies who rode sidesaddle in earlier days carried a crop or small whip to tap the horse on that side – to give the signals you'd ordinarily give with that leg. I used a willow stick as my riding crop, to give gentle taps where my leg would have been, and Khamette had to get used to that new signal!

After a bit of practice, however, we got good at it and I found that by gripping the two curving horns between my legs I had a secure, seat, even for jumping. I could post the trot and keep my body square and well balanced at all gaits, handling Khamette almost as well as when riding astride. We practiced all kinds of maneuvers at all gaits.

Our big test was riding sidesaddle in the Salmon River Days' Parade in early July. Our Salmon church was celebrating its 90th anniversary and members were participating in various exhibits in the parade, portraying the early days of the church. The Ravndals wore old-style clothing from the 1800s and rode in their old buggy, pulled by their two gray mares. My father rode Nell, wearing an old black suit and hat, dressed like Brother

Van, the famous circuit rider who started our church and other churches in western Montana, riding hundreds of miles between congregations to preach. I borrowed an old long dress from one of the older ladies and wore my hair in a style like 90 years earlier.

Dad helped me mount, since it's hard to get on a horse with a long dress! Khamette was nervous and pranced a little during the parade with all the people lining the streets, but did well for a young green ranch horse that had never experienced anything like this.

The rest of the summer flew by, doing our ranch chores. We had a little wreck later that summer but it wasn't her fault. A few lazy range cows had come down out of the hills and found a bad patch of fence where the county road-grader had pushed over one of the posts, and it was almost flat on the ground. I discovered them in the hayfield while riding Khamette and tried to chase them out. We were doing a good job, galloping after one ornery cow who tried to run the wrong direction. Then Khamette hit a slippery spot – a patch of mud from the irrigation water – just as she was making a tight turn after the cow. Her legs went out from under her and she fell down on her side. I was thrown clear, skidding along in the grass a few feet away from the fallen horse.

We both had scrapes and bruises; Khamette lost some hair off one knee and my arm was scraped, but nothing serious. I got up as she was scrambling to her feet so I grabbed the reins and got back on, and we took off after the cow again. This time we got her headed the right direction and brought her back to the rest of the group, and got them out the gate. We herded the cows back up the draw to the range, then came back and propped up the post where they got over the fence.

HORSE TALES

It wasn't until we started home that I discovered I'd lost my watch. I glanced at my wrist to see how late it was getting, and realized I didn't have it. I'd broken it when I landed on the ground. I rode back up to the field and found the skid marks in the grass. I dismounted and searched around, and found the watch – with a broken band.

Then I was off to college again for my sophomore year at University of Puget Sound in Tacoma, Washington. The worst thing about going to college was missing my horses, and the ranch. The summer of 1964 when I got home from college, I was eager to continue riding Khamette, and start training Nikki, my two-year-old filly. But in July that year my dad took another church parish (after spending 18 years at Salmon as preacher of the Salmon Methodist Church) and we moved to Laurel, Montana. Dad leased the ranch (and sold the cattle) to another rancher. I had a small herd that I'd been building up for several years, and those were sold, too, since I no longer had a place to keep them. We sold all our horses except Nell, and my two (Khamette and Nikki). Jerry Ravndal hauled them to Laurel for us. We found a rancher near town who could pasture the horses.

That summer Khamette was five and I rode her a lot – trotting on the back roads. I was really homesick, and riding was the best way to ease the ache of not being able to ride range in the mountains I loved. All that trotting on hard-packed dirt roads took a toll, and Khamette developed splints on both front legs. Even though splints are more common in two- and three-year-olds (from too much work and concussion), the splint bone isn't fully attached to the cannon bone until a horse is about five. With Khamette's offset cannon bones there was more stress on the inner splint bone directly under the knee, and she developed bony enlargements. After the initial inflammation and tenderness, however, she was no longer lame, and the splints were merely a bony lump under each knee.

That summer I was so homesick for the ranch, with no range to ride, that I channeled that frustrated energy into writing my first book (*A Horse in Your Life: A Guide for the New Owner*). I illustrated it with sketches and photos. Khamette posed for most of the photos, and I hired my brother to take pictures – showing how to saddle and bridle a horse, mount and dismount, groom a horse, pick up and clean feet, trim feet, lead a horse properly, etc. She was my first foal, my first training project from start to finish, my guinea pig for all my new ideas, including a book!

KHAMETTE'S LATER YEARS
From Cow Horse to Kid Horse

After my family moved to Laurel, Montana in 1964, I went back to University of Puget Sound for my junior year, majoring in English and history. My horses spent the winter on a ranch near Redlodge, running in a pasture next to cattle and bison. The rancher did some crossbreeding, and during Christmas vacation I rode Khamette in those big pastures and enjoyed seeing the bison, and some of the crossbreds. The rancher had two in his corrals, getting ready to butcher. One was ¾ Angus, ¼ bison and jet black, with a hump and horns. A huge whiteface steer (half bison, half Hereford) was red and shaggy. Khamette was curious about these strange animals but we didn't get very close to the bison in the pastures because they were wild and unpredictable.

Those were tough years. I was miserabe in the city, going to college, and a fish out of water at my family's home at Laurel, missing the ranch. I decided to go to summer school at UPS the summer of 1965, to take enough courses to finish college early – after the first semester of senior year – and get on with my life.

I had gone to UPS to please my parents, but I really wanted to spend my life with horses and cattle. If I couldn't ranch, I planned to do the next best thing – study veterinary medicine. In the 1960s, very few women were accepted into vet school, so my plan was to graduate from UPS and then go to Montana State University at Bozeman, and take pre-vet courses. I figured I could learn how to doctor my own horses and cattle – if I ever had a chance to own cattle again. Maybe I would meet a young rancher going to college at Bozeman!

Fate intervened. The book I wrote during the summer of 1964 was accepted by A.S. Barnes & Company and published in 1966. There was an article in the Salmon newspaper (*Recorder Herald*) in February 1965, telling about my book being accepted for publication. That news item changed my life.

I was a very shy person growing up, and hadn't dated any boys in high school (and just a couple "sort of" dates in college). Salmon was a small town, with a small school, and everyone knew everybody else. There was a boy in the class ahead of me, Lynn Thomas, who was friendly and nice, but we were both too shy to become friends. His family had a ranch north of town, and he's the one who sold Scrappy to my dad in 1957 – when I was between seventh and eighth grade – when we needed another ranch horse.

Ironically, that mare became the mother of my beloved Khamette, and that boy later became my husband. In 1965 he was in a partnership with his older brother on a dairy farm near Gooding, Idaho (and raising a few Angus cattle), and working part-time for a carpenter-cabinet maker. His brother Bill and sister-in-law Nita still subscribed to the *Recorder Herald*. Nita saw the news item about my book being published, and showed it to Lynn. "Isn't this one of your old schoolmates? You ought to look her up!"

The news item mentioned I was attending University of Puget Sound, in Tacoma. It just so happened that the cabinet maker had to make a trip to the Seattle area in March, and invited Lynn to go along. Lynn's brother had recently attended a bull sale in Denver and was gone for five days and Lynn had to take care of the dairy while he was gone. It was his turn to take a trip!

So Lynn went with his carpenter friend, and they stopped in Tacoma to see me. I was really surprised to see this young man from home, and even more surprised to discover how comfortable I felt with him. He was so easy to be with, and we had similar backgrounds and enjoyed the same things. We began writing letters – through the rest of that school year and while I was at summer school. Then during the last week of summer school, I became very sick with a virus and had to fly home, ending up in the hospital in Billings, Montana for two weeks, on IV fluids. Lynn came to visit me in the hospital and gave me an engagement ring (he literally caught me at a weak moment!) and we got married the next March.

I was finished with college by then, staying with my folks at Laurel. We had the wedding in Salmon, since that was our "home town." Lynn stayed with his folks, and my family and I stayed with old friends. After the wedding, instead of a honeymoon, Lynn and I went home to the dairy farm at Gooding to milk the cows. By that time he'd ended the partnership with his brother, split the cow herd, and rented another small dairy farm.

Khamette, Nikki and Nell were still pastured near Laurel until my parents moved back to the ranch at Salmon that summer. Dad took a year off from pastoring a church, and taught government in the Salmon high school. They moved the horses back to our ranch, even though the fields and range were still leased out to

Lynn on Bambi and me on Khamette in 1967.

the rancher who bought our cows. So Khamette was back on the ranch again, in the pasture where she grew up.

Lynn and I spent that summer on the rented dairy farm at Gooding, milking cows and raising a few calves and pigs, then sold the milk cows that fall. We loaded up our few belongings (and Lynn's horse and Angus cow and calf, and some dairy heifers) and came back to the ranch in November 1966. We leased my folks' place (and later bought it), and started buying the ranch below it. So my horses and I were back on the creek again, home again at last and forever.

The winter of 1966-67, Khamette and our other horses were pastured on our 320. I kept Nikki down here at the ranch so I'd have a horse to ride and be able to check on the other horses. One day mid-winter I rode up to the 320 and discovered that Khamette was lame on her right front foot, and she'd lost weight. She apparently hadn't been traveling much to graze or go to water, and was almost impacted; her manure was small, firm balls.

I led her home and checked the bottom of her foot more closely. It looked like a puncture wound in the sole that had abscessed. I opened it up a little more with a hoof knife so it could drain, and then soaked her foot in a bucket of hot water and Epsom salts. I put her in the pen with Nikki where she could have plenty of hay and water. By the next day she was walking better, and eating more. After a few more daily soaking sessions she was no longer lame.

On subsequent rides to the 320 I looked around for anything that might have created a puncture wound in her foot, because it was a very safe mountain pasture. There had been an old homestead shack up there at one time, however, and I searched through the sagebrush at that site and found some old boards with nails in them. Mystery solved. We gathered those up, so no horse or cow could puncture a foot again.

The spring of 1967 Lynn and I borrowed money and purchased some Hereford heifers from a rancher across the valley. My dad bought another group from that same rancher, and we leased those from him and bred all the heifers to Angus bulls. We also bought 40 pregnant Angus and crossbred heifers from a cow buyer at Gooding, and they calved that summer. We bought 19 Angus and crossbred cows (with calves at side) from a local rancher. So we had cattle on the range again and I rode nearly every day to check on them and make sure the water troughs were working. I usually rode Khamette or Nikki (my younger mare), or Bambi (the mare Lynn bought just before we left Gooding).

Our son Michael was born the next spring – April 15, 1968. My little sister was 12 years old that year (she was 12 years younger than me) and often helped us ride range, and enjoyed riding Khamette.

Two weeks after I got out of the hospital having Michael, I put shoes on Khamette for my sister to ride. At that point in time, I was very glad that Khamette was always easy to shoe!

The next year my folks lived in Choteau, Montana (where dad was pastoring a church that needed a preacher), and my sis came to spend the summer with us, helping with chores, riding range, and taking care of Michael, who was a year old. She and I usually rode Khamette and Nikki to check cattle. One day Lynn and I were moving cows, however, and she was staying home babysitting. The cattle gather took longer than anticipated. It got to be late evening, chores needed to be done – milking the cow, letting the calves in to the nurse cow, etc. and Heidi realized we wouldn't be back in time. She took Michael out to the barn in the back pack that I carried him around in, and hung it on the old log barn wall out of harm's way while she milked the cow and fed the calves.

The summer of 1968, Jerry and Velma Ravndal put on the first Salmon River Trail Ride – a 40-mile competitive ride that the horses had to complete in five-and-a-half to six hours. It was part of the Rocky Mountain Trail Ride Conference, which by then was a group of six rides in Montana, Idaho and Wyoming. Riders could compete in their division (junior, lightweight or heavyweight) in three or more rides to vie for end-of-year conference championships. Those awards were given out each year at the final 60-mile Bitterroot Ride near Hamilton, Montana.

The Salmon River Ride made a 40-mile loop from the Fairgrounds – out through the foothills and into the mountains and back, and went through our cattle range. In 1970, we let them have their noon check stop in a meadow at the upper end of our ranch. The day of the ride, Heidi was riding Khamette checking cows on our high range. She saw the riders trotting down the old jeep road, so she followed them and came trotting into the noon stop. Jerry Ravndal looked at Khamette, who took about two deep breaths after a five-mile trot, and said this mare was in better shape than most of the competitors and that Heidi should have entered her in the competition.

So that was her plan for the next summer. When Heidi came to stay with us (arriving end of May) she rode range nearly every day. The one setback was a saddle sore that had begun the fall before, on both sides of Khamette's backbone in the cantle area. It may have been caused by too much pressure. The child's saddle she'd been riding was no longer big enough for her, and the short bars were pressing too hard into Khamette's back. The rubbing pressure was aggravated by our stiff hair pads.

We had to get the sore healed up before the trail ride in July. Heidi switched to a bigger saddle, but realized that in order for the sore to heal it needed some time without pressure and rubbing of any saddle and pad. She rode Khamette most of the summer bareback to let it heal so she could use a saddle on the trail ride, since one of the rules was that the rider must use a saddle.

Heidi was already a good rider, but those two months riding bareback made her an excellent rider – chasing cows, galloping downhill, jumping over logs and sagebrush. The only thing she worried about were rattlesnakes. Our other horses didn't worry about snakes but Khamette was afraid of them after having been bitten as a filly. She'd react instantly, if she heard one, spinning away from it. She could spin 180 degrees in a flash. Heidi always worried about the possibility of that mare leaping away from a snake, spinning out from under her and dumping her right onto the snake!

The sore healed and Heidi was able to use a saddle. We created a soft pad using foam rubber and an outer covering made from a doubled wool army blanket, with a soft, wool baby blanket stitched on the side next to the horse. She used that pad for the 40-mile ride that year (1971), and did very well, placing second in the junior division and fifth place in Junior Horsemanship. The saddle sore didn't open up (or it would have disqualified her). Later we bought some of the new fleece pads made of synthetic material that hospitals use for bedridden patients to prevent pressure sores.

Khamette was probably one of the best horses we ever had for traveling lots of miles, with her smooth, fast trot. She was great to ride range on and cover the country in a hurry. One time Heidi and I were coming home from riding range and moving cows, hurrying to get back home in time to go to a friend's wedding, and we were late. We had to cover the last six miles (coming down out of the steep mountains) in a very short time. We trotted all the way, at a very fast trot. Usually our horses cool out pretty well at a trot coming home down these trails but we'd had a long hard cattle drive plus the hurry home and the horses were still sweaty when we arrived at the barnyard. We didn't put them away immediately because we didn't want them to tank up on cold water. So we let them graze a few moments in the front yard while we rushed into the house and quickly washed the trail dust off our arms and faces, changed into dresses and hurried back out to put the horses away. They had never seen us in dresses and looked startled as we came running out to the yard, but as soon as we spoke to them they realized it was just us.

My sis rode Khamette each summer she spent with us, until she bought an Arabian stallion named Surrabu and started riding him – the summer before she went to college the fall of 1972. Our son

HORSE TALES

Michael rode Khamette a few times when he was three, but more regularly when he was four. I led Khamette from my horse because the kid was still too little to be the pilot. His stubby legs didn't reach below the saddle pad and she couldn't feel him kicking, and he wasn't quite strong enough to keep her from putting her head down to grab grass along the way. She quickly figured out that it was easy to graze when packing this little guy.

Lynn or one of the neighbors could sometimes look after our younger daughter, so I often took Michael with me when I rode range, leading Khamette from my horse, until he graduated to riding her solo. He was about five or six years old when he was helping move cows on a windy day. The cows kicked loose a piece of sagebrush and it blew toward Khamette. She whirled and left him sitting on the ground. I think that's the only time he ever fell off her.

Our daughter Andrea was born in 1970, and she started riding Khamette on a lead line. By then Michael was riding Brownie and I could take both kids along to ride range while Lynn was busy with irrigation and haying. With a kid on Khamette, led from my horse (Nikki) chasing cows was doable. That mare led so well that we could trot or gallop after a cow, the horses side by side if terrain permitted, or single file if we had to weave through tall sagebrush or go through the timber. She was the best kid horse! Both kids learned to herd cattle early on, and were proud of their accomplishment when they could ride Khamette to chase cows without mom leading her.

Andrea fell off one time when we'd been riding all day and coming home from the high range. We'd forgotten to check Andrea's cinch, and when I opened the gate to start home, Khamette dropped her head down to graze after Andrea rode her through the gate. The cinch was so loose and the saddle so far

Michael, age four, riding Khamette solo.

forward after coming down the mountain, that Andrea, saddle and all slipped down over the mare's head.

Andrea landed on the ground in front of the mare. The saddle was halfway down Khamette's neck, with the cinch around her front legs, hobbling her head to her front legs! But she didn't panic, she just kept enjoying the opportunity to eat grass until I was able to undo the cinch and put the saddle onto her back again.

Khamette was completely gentle and trustworthy but her one fault was the fact she didn't like strange horses coming up behind her and bumping her. She had a tendency to kick. On one range ride our neighbor Bill Sager was helping move cows and kept ramming the cattle with his horse, and ramming up behind Andrea's horse. She kept warning him that Khamette might kick, but he didn't think the gentle old mare would do that. He rammed right into her, and sure enough, she kicked at his horse and hit Bill

121

on the knee. Fortunately she didn't break his knee.

Her kick was noteworthy on one other occasion. Andrea was on Khamette helping us move cows and we had our old dog with us. Pepper wasn't a very brave cowdog and usually stayed behind our horses. Even though we could send her after a wayward cow, she'd give up quickly if it turned around to face her. We had some Angus cows that didn't like dogs, and that day one of them (named Joan) bellowed and chased Pepper, who ran up behind and under Khamette for safety, with Joan right on her tail. Khamette just stood there calmly and whacked Joan in the face with one hind foot. That halted the cow right in her tracks. She went off shaking her head and left the dog alone.

In 1971 Jerry Ravndal died, and Velma had to sell their little ranch and most of their Arabian horses. We boarded several horses here for a few years, and kept three of her old mares (that she continued to ride, coming out here to the ranch to ride range with us). We kept a young Arabian stallion here through the summer of 1972. His name was Sur Amir, and Velma and Jerry had raised him to breed to their El Khamis daughters. While he was here, we bred three of our mares to him – Khamette, Nikki (El Khamis daughters), and Bambi (Lynn's Quarter Horse mare).

Khamette was 13 at that time, and this would be her first foal. She foaled April 28, 1973 – a chestnut filly that we named Khamir. Having her first foal at age 14 was a bit old for a first-time mama. The foal was big, and the middle-aged mare's pelvis was probably not as pliant as that of a younger mare. Lynn and I gave Khamette a little help and pulled the foal because Khamette was taking so long. The next problem was that she had very little milk. The filly nursed almost constantly, through that first day of life, until Khamette finally came to her milk. She was a good mama, however, and raised a good filly. We never bred her again, because we didn't want to risk having anything happen to that mare. She was much too valuable as a kid horse and spare ranch horse, so that was the only year we let her raise a baby.

I'd been riding some of our younger horses on the Rocky Mountain Conference rides for several years, and when Michael became old enough to compete he had his heart set on riding his horse Brownie on our Salmon River Ride. The kids helped me mark trail that year, riding Brownie and Khamette. The night before the ride, Michael camped at the ride site at the upper end of our ranch with his grandpa (my dad, who would also be riding). By then the "noon stop" had become the campground where the ride began and ended, since the Fairgrounds had been moved to the other side of town and was no longer feasible. We'd solved that problem by making a 20-mile loop through the mountains near our ranch – with the riders traveling one way in the morning and then doing the loop backward in the afternoon.

Sometime during the night Brownie got loose and tried to come home down the back side of our ranch, and got caught in an old fence, cutting his shoulder severely. We did a hurried search that next morning and found him stranded, and led him home to treat his wounds. Michael was devastated, so we grabbed Khamette out of her pasture and quickly substituted – and he was still able to do the trail ride on her. Even though she was getting old she did the ride just fine.

Wire cuts seem to be the biggest hazard for horses on a lot of western ranches where barbed-wire fences are the norm for cattle.

Khamette tangled with some old wire herself, when I was riding her on one of our leased pastures and found some stray range cattle that had come through a fence. I started to head them toward a gate and they tried to run to the brush in the creek bottom. I dashed through a small opening in the brush to head them off and got into some old barbed wire – from a fence that had long since fallen down and been overgrown by brush. One strand of the wire was still firmly attached to old posts that were flat on the ground.

When Khamette's foot hit the wire she spooked backward, catching her pastern on the solidly anchored piece. I tried to urge her forward but in her panic she kept pulling backward, sawing her front foot deeply and slicing an artery before she pulled free. When I jumped off to check the damage, it was spurting blood – as high as her belly.

I had a stretchy nylon sweater tied to my saddle. I quickly wrapped it tightly around her pastern to slow the bleeding, then led her the three miles home. Later that day we trailered her to the vet, and he put a plaster cast on her lower leg (covering the hoof and extending to just below her knee) to hold the edges of the gash together until it healed. When we took the cast off a few weeks later it had healed nicely, with very little scar. Meanwhile, we gathered up all that old fence wire, dragging it out of the brush, like we gathered up the old fence that Brownie got into when he tried to go home from the trail ride camp.

In 1980, Andrea rode Khamette on the Salmon Ride and placed second in the novice division, and received an award for being the youngest rider (10) on the oldest horse (21). The old mare carried her effortlessly and enjoyed every mile.

In 1982 – when Andrea was 12 – we had a summer guest who

rode Khamette. Penny was the daughter of our landlord (he owned one of the ranches next to ours, and we leased it for 40 years). Penny lived in a big city and wanted to know what it was like to live on a ranch. She spent two weeks with us and rode Khamette whenever we rode range. By that time Andrea was riding Khamir (Khamette's daughter) and Brownie (Michael's horse) so Khamette was mainly the "spare" horse that anybody could ride.

Penny rode many miles on Khamette and saw lots of wildlife (including a couple of bighorn sheep, which are normally not found on our range). She had one accident, however, when we forgot to check her cinch, and the saddle slipped down on Khamette's neck while going down a steep hill – depositing Penny on the ground. It's times like that when a person really appreciates a truly dependable kid horse!

Khamette was the horse everybody and anybody could ride – all our guests and relatives that came to visit – and she give them a safe and enjoyable ride. My twin cousin Diane (who rode with me on old Possum when we were kids) came to visit during those years, and she rode Khamette. Those were good times, good memories!

In the last years of her life, the old mare had arthritic joints – especially her knees, and they became stiffer. She became a lot more crippled after she was 25, the year we retired her from riding. We realized too late that exercise was the best thing for those old joints. Inactivity made them worse. So with sadness, and gratitude for all she'd done for our family, and fond memories of the early years when she was my first "baby," I led her out into the hills she loved, on one of our hill pastures, and we put her gently to sleep. I like to envision her spirit trotting happily over those hills.

NIKKI
My Best Cow Horse

When a door slams shuts, another opens. When our Thoroughbred mare Nell lost her first foal, Amahl, at a month of age – from a scrotal hernia – we rebred her that summer to the same little Arabian stallion, El Khamis. My 4-H leaders felt badly that I'd lost the foal of my dreams, and rebred my mare at no charge. That fall Nell suffered severe cuts on both front legs when she went through a fence. For several days she was too lame to walk and spent most of her time lying down. I worried about her health, and the unborn foal she was carrying. I treated her wounds until they healed enough (in late November) to take her to winter pasture.

In late February I brought Nell down from the mountains and started feeding her hay and grain. By mid-May she was started to develop some udder, so I cleaned out the old stackyard and put her in there at nights where I could check on her. The filly that arrived at midnight, May 30, 1962, the same week I graduated from high school, became my once-in-a-lifetime very best cowhorse.

I named her Nokomis, but she quickly became "Nikki". She was a feisty little filly and had a strong mind of her own as I was teaching her to lead and tie, but she soon figured out that the rope was stronger than she was. I spent a lot of time with her that summer before I went to college, and she was always easy to handle after that. When I went off to college (in Tacoma, Washington) I was terribly homesick – missing my horses. In my letters home I always asked about them.

Dad weaned the filly for me, and she lived in the big corral by the creek. I came home for Thanksgiving that year, even though it was a short vacation and hardly worth the day-long train ride both directions (to Missoula, Montana, 140 miles from home, where my parents came to pick me up, and then take me back), but I got to see my horses. Later that winter Nikki injured a knee. Dad described it in a letter to me; perhaps she ran into something in the corral. My dad treated it for several weeks. I worried that it might damage the joint, but she healed ok and was sound.

The summer of 1963 Nikki led a carefree life as a yearling with our other horses. I worked with her periodically, leading her, tying her up, trimming her feet. I wanted her to be well-mannered when she grew up. Then my family moved to Laurel, Montana, in 1964. Jerry Ravndal hauled Nell, Nikki and Khamette to Laurel, the two mares in his horse trailer, and Nikki in the back of his pickup in a rack he built. We kept the horses on a ranch near Laurel for the two years my folks lived there. That's where I started her saddling lessons and trained her. I started riding her that summer as a long two-year-old.

Toward the end of that summer I put on her first set of shoes. I took my shoeing tools out to the ranch where she was pastured, but forgot to take my chaps. Nikki never tried to take a foot away, so I didn't really need them. I have a pair of very old, heavy leather chaps that I wear when shoeing horses, to protect my legs. A nail sticking out the side of the foot might go through the leather if the horse jerked a foot, but wouldn't poke into my leg. I was proud of Nikki, being so good to shoe for the first time.

Nikki stayed on the ranch near Laurel until the summer of 1966. Lynn and I were married in March that year and were on a dairy farm at Gooding, and my dad brought her to Gooding later that summer. I used her to gather the heifers after they went through a fence into our alfalfa field. That was the first chance she'd ever had to work cattle, and I realized she was going to be a natural at handling cattle.

That summer we were short of pasture. We kept our two horses in a small pasture where they watered in an irrigation ditch, and staked them out in the barnyard when they ran out of grass. Nikki was smart and figured out the stake rope pretty quickly. She only got tangled once, and was calm about letting me get her untangled.

One day I noticed she was holding her left eye partly closed. It looked blue and was watering, sensitive to sunlight. I assumed she injured it in brush. A few days later the eye seemed fine.

At the end of the year we moved back to Salmon. We had a farm sale and sold the dairy cows – all but two springer heifers we'd just bought. We kept them and a few heifer calves and made the trip back home. It was quite a move, with borrowed trucks and help from Dad and neighbors, hauling cattle, horses, tractors, calves, dog and cats!

We were ready to make the switch from dairy farmers to ranchers. We stayed with my parents a few weeks until Bob and Wilma Grounds moved out of their little house on the ranch we were going to buy. We moved into that house after Christmas – a log cabin built by the original homesteaders in 1885. Bob and Wilma were selling their place – half of it to us and half to people from Georgia who had purchased the Gooch place (the other small ranch on the creek). Things were

Nikki and me me moving cattle.

quite different from when my family left the creek three years earlier.

That spring we built a fence to divide the Grounds place – our portion that included the house and barns, and the lower field that would belong to the new neighbor. Some of the other fences were old and not very functional, and we had numerous episodes that summer with the neighbors' cows getting into our hayfields. One day a cow got in and I ran to get Nikki and didn't take time to go saddle her. I jumped on bareback with just a halter and went galloping after the cow when she headed the wrong direction. I beat her to the fence to turn her the right way, and Nikki slid to a stop at the fence but I didn't – I went over her head still hanging onto the halter rope, landing on my back on the tight new barbed wire fence. Like a tight rubber band, it bounced me up off the wire and I landed on my feet, still holding onto the rope. My guardian angel was on duty; if I'd landed on a post instead of the wire it would have broken my back. Unhurt, I jumped on Nikki bareback again and finished herding the cow out of our field.

We had neighbor problems for two years until that family went broke and moved. That ranch was owned by an older brother who lived in a city, and after his family moved he leased it to us – for 40 years. By putting together the three little ranches on our creek, we could increase our cow herd enough to try to make a living.

As Nikki and I did more cattle work that first summer, I realized she was the most agile horse I'd ever ridden, quick as a cat (like her mother Nell), and she loved chasing cows as much as I did. She gave it her all, and I had to really be "with it" to stay on her when she was after a cow. If it changed direction, she did, too, and I'd better be paying attention. She had a sixth sense when we worked through a herd, sorting. Whenever I found the cow I needed, or calf that had to be sorted out to go with its mama, she knew which one I was looking at, and she'd focus on it until we got it out of the herd.

I never worried about footing (ice, snow, frozen hillsides, bogs) because she could maneuver through anything while sorting a herd or chasing a cow. For many years I rode her in the early winter to check cows on our 320-acre mountain pasture, and to bring them home when the snow got too deep. I used Nikki to sort out heavies during calving season, easing them out of the herd in the field below our land, and into the maternity pen. She spoiled me, because she could keep her balance in icy conditions. I never had another horse I trusted quite as much on slippery footing (though Nell was also very surefooted), and after Nikki was gone we didn't use a horse to sort the pregnant cows. We did it on foot. By that time, however, our cows were well trained to be handled on foot as well as horseback.

The first summer on the ranch, with Lynn riding his Quarter Horse mare Bambi and me on Nikki we had a few friendly (perhaps childish!) arguments about which was the best horse, or the fastest. Nikki was as agile and quick as Bambi cutting cows, and more surefooted, but we still argued about speed. One day we had a silly race. We were on our way home from riding range, coming down the creek road. There was a long straight stretch going up a slight grade, with good footing, so we had a horse race. Bambi had a slightly faster takeoff and led the way for the first 100 yards, then Nikki passed her. As we topped the grade and the road made a corner, we were going so fast that we ended up off the road in the sagebrush. I was afraid we might hit the fence, so I bailed off, and landed on my shoulder and hurt my elbow. We had invited Lynn's folks for dinner that day and I had to cook dinner with that arm in a sling!

Nikki was high spirited and hyper, always eager to go, and might be a little goofy sometimes, but if we had a cow job to do she was instantly focused; she funneled all that energy into working the cows. She might be prancing and dancing at the first part of a ride if I hadn't ridden her for a couple months, but as soon as we got to the cows she was cool, calm and collected and ready for work. I could always trust her to be my willing partner for tough jobs.

She had a lot of heart and gave it her all. When you have a horse like that, always part of the team, always working her heart out for you, all you can do is humbly accept that loyalty with gratitude. I loved that mare, but I did nothing to deserve such dedication. I always felt like she was the best part of the team effort. In later years I've trained and ridden many horses, but none with quite as much talent and desire. She had the athletic ability, agility and heart to do any job, and enjoyed doing it. But for a while we didn't know if she'd have a future.

That first summer after we moved back to the ranch, Nikki's eye suddenly became dull blue, with impaired vision. The veterinarian who examined it thought she'd injured it and advised me to put her in a dark barn and apply antibiotic eye ointment several times a day, which I did. There was a log barn on the ranch and we cleaned it out and put her in there, out of the sunlight.

The eye didn't get better, and Nikki was going stir crazy in the barn. So I let her back out in the pasture, but fastened a folded towel to her halter on that side – to protect that eye from sunlight. This was before the days of fly masks. She wore the halter and eye patch whenever the "attacks" became worse and the eye was sensitive to bright light. Finally I had another veterinarian examine the eye. He diagnosed it as periodic ophthalmia (moon blindness, now called recurrent uveitis) and told me it was caused by leptospirosis – after he took blood tests to check her titer for lepto. We'd vaccinated our cattle against this disease, but I'd never heard of it in horses.

I did some research on leptospirosis and learned it affects many species – humans, dogs, livestock and horses. This disease often affects the kidneys and is caused by spiral-shaped bacteria. There are many kinds of pathogenic leptospires and most have preferred hosts; certain types are found most commonly in dogs, pigs or rats, for instance. Pathogens are often found in wildlife, including deer, rats and mice. Leptospires can survive in surface water, stagnant ponds, or streams.

Lepto is spread by discharges and secretions (especially urine) of sick and carrier animals, which often contaminate feed and water. Some infected animals appear to be healthy, yet harbor the bacteria in their kidneys and reproductive tract, shedding these bacteria in urine or reproductive fluids. Bacteria may enter a susceptible animal via nose, mouth or eyes by contact with contaminated feed, water or urine. Once the leptospires enter an animal, they multiply in the liver and migrate through the bloodstream to the kidneys; they release

Nikki and baby Nikkolis in 1973.

toxins that damage red blood cells, liver and kidneys.

Even though leptospirosis is often a mild disease in horses, secondary effects may have serious consequences. These include abortion in pregnant mares, and sometimes eye problems (recurrent uveitis). In retrospect, I realized that Nikki probably encountered this disease the summer before (when she had her first episode), while Lynn and I were leasing the small farm. We had dairy cows and pigs, and our horses were in a pasture serviced by an irrigation ditch that came through many farms. One of our sows aborted her piglets that summer, and the diagnosis was leptospirosis.

During the summer of 1967 Lynn and I doctored Nikki with everything our local vet could think of that might help, giving her countless injections of vitamins, and several types of daily injections of medication including a non-specific protein treatment that was supposed to help clear up the cloudiness in her eye. I tried to learn everything I could about leptospirosis and "moonblindness" to find the best way to treat her, and protect our other horses. For several years we vaccinated our horses with the cattle vaccine. It was difficult to find accurate information, and frustrating; veterinarians had vastly different opinions. One thought my mare should be put down; he claimed she'd be a carrier of lepto for the rest of her life. So I began a desperate search for facts about this disease, and was grateful to several veterinarians and researchers around the country who were able to give me advice at a time it was sorely needed.

The eye varied in its usefulness that summer. Sometimes she had vision, sometimes not. In late summer she was totally blind in that eye. I had to be careful when approaching her on that side, always speaking to her, so my touch would not startle her. By fall the eye began to improve and I was able to ride her again. She was my best cow horse and I needed her for cattle work. We continued giving the vitamin shots every two weeks through fall and winter. As a young filly, Nikki had been very sensitive about "shots," resisting injections, but through this ordeal she became very accepting.

Even though she could see again, her vision was still impaired in dim light. She was spooky on her bad side when coming home from a long range ride after dark. Her eye remained cloudy for more than a year and I was afraid she might go blind, but she never had another episode.

When she was nine (in 1971) I rode her on the 40-mile Salmon River Ride, and she did well, but I rode her younger sister Fahleen on the next year's ride and bred Nikki. By that time she could take time off to have a foal because I was riding Fahleen to do much of the range riding, and I wanted to raise at least one foal from Nikki before she became too old. We leased a stallion that year and bred four mares

— Nell, Nikki, Bambi, Khamette. Nell didn't settle, but the other mares were pregnant, to foal in 1973.

Nikki had a nice bay colt, and even though he was three-quarters Arab he threw back to his Thoroughbred grandmother and that branch of the family for size. Nikki was only 14.3 hands, and her son Nikkolis grew up to be taller and leggier at 15.3 hands.

We tried a couple more times to breed Nikki — once to an Arabian in our valley, and once to an Arabian in Boise — but she didn't settle. For the rest of her life she was my best horse. Even when I was riding younger horses, if there was a tough sorting job to do, or cattle work in treacherous footing, Nikki was the one I'd choose. The only time she ever fell down was during an emergency calf roundup one icy winter when she was 24 years old and getting a little stiff. We were galloping across the snow and ice on the Gooch place in early March, bringing home an orphan calf. When Lynn and I went up there to feed cows that morning, we found Laura dead in the ditch. She'd gotten on her back, bloated and died — leaving a six-week-old calf. We went back home and I got Nikki, to bring the calf home to raise on our milk cow.

I'd sorted the calf into a little group of cows and calves to bring down to the main ranch. The orphan was reluctantly coming along, but kept trying to go back to her dead mama. Everything was going smoothly until the calf darted away and ran back up the field. Nikki and I sprinted to head her off, and hit an icy slope — and her feet went out from under her. I fell clear and we went skidding along on the ice. We picked ourselves up and started over, getting the orphan into another group of cows and calves, and this time we got her clear home. I realized that the old mare wasn't quite as agile anymore.

I still rode her to sort cows; she was my best cutting horse in the corral. But age was catching up with her. She'd always been sensitive to dusty hay, and I'd have to shake it up and sprinkle it, or she'd cough. In old age she'd developed a more severe sensitivity, especially to dusty alfalfa, so I was careful about what I fed her.

Most of our horses were kept in drylots and fed hay, even in summer, rather than pasture. I saved the pasture for mares and foals. The hard-working horses did better (and kept their condition better) on good grass hay rather than washy green pasture. In their pens I could also feed each one as an individual – feeding more to the ones that needed it and less to the easy keepers who just got fatter. I could feed the least dusty hay to Nikki, to keep her from coughing. She had one severe breathing episode and needed medication (steroids) to open her airways, so I made sure she never got any more dusty alfalfa hay.

Then during late winter 1988 I was gone for a while, for a double mastectomy. Some of our hay that year was dusty (rained on before we got it baled). I had carefully sorted the hay before I left, leaving a pile for Nikki, so Lynn and Andrea could easily do my horse chores for me. But I was gone a few more days than anticipated, due to complications, and my chore crew ran out of hay for Nikki. They did their best to sort out hay for her, but when I got home she was wheezing and struggling to breathe.

The weather was nasty and cold, which made her even more miserable, and I wasn't in very good shape for treating her. I hated to see her suffering so much – my brave little mare. So I made the painful decision to put her down. We buried her in the bull corral, since it was the only place on the ranch where the ground wasn't frozen. So I lost my good mare at age 26 and felt that I'd failed her--by being gone, by not being strong enough to nurse her through her bad time when I got back. But at that point in her life, release from her agony seemed to be the kindest thing I could do.

FAHLEEN
The Clown

I had her for only seven years, but in that short time she changed my life. She was a chestnut Arab-Thoroughbred mare named Fahleen. A clown, a sassy, naughty redhead, she had a unique sense of humor and tremendous athletic ability; she was one of the best range-riding long-distance horse I ever owned, with a lot of heart.

She came into my life on a cold day in March 1967 (exactly a year after my husband Lynn and I were married), a wobbly-legged filly with an irregular marking on her face. She was very independent and often exasperating to handle. Her Thoroughbred mother, Nell, came from a long line of very independent equines and Fahleen was a challenge to train. I had to earn her respect. In reality, she was training me.

As time went on, she came to accept and tolerate me, and then to think of me as sort of a second mother, trusting me as completely as I trusted her. After I'd ridden her for a couple years, our relationship was well grounded in trust. I could do anything with her that she considered reasonable, and we were a team.

HORSE TALES

Our first years together, however, were very trying, partly because of her unique sense of humor. She was more like a big monkey than a horse, doing all kinds of un-horse-like activities to entertain herself. She'd often toss her grain tub into the air, or fling the water hose over her head for fun. She beat on her water tank with a front foot if it wasn't full enough to suit her. I had to use a metal tank because she thought rubber tubs were just for playing soccer. Sometimes she'd take the top strand of fence wire in her teeth and pluck it like a banjo string, just to hear the sound it made.

She was bold and curious. When she was young, there was only an electric wire separating her part of the pasture from our hayfields. If the electricity went off, she immediately knew it, and walked over or under the wire. She wasn't afraid of anything, and would walk out on the ice-covered creek in the winter without hesitation.

Her boldness sometimes got her into trouble, like trying to open gates with her front feet. When she was 4 she got her foot caught in a gate, and by the time she pulled free, she had injured the joints in her lower leg. The leg swelled up as big as a fencepost, in spite of the cold water and ice I soaked it in (using a tall home-made soaking boot created from a rubber inner tube, held in place with a leather strap over her back). She could hardly walk for several days. I had to lay her off for the rest of that riding season.

The leg healed but the pastern joint fused as it healed, leaving the joint solid (no movement) and a calcium lump on the side of it. When I started riding her again, I discovered that the fused pastern joint made the action in that leg a little different. Not only was there limited motion in the pastern, making her stride a little shorter on that leg (and landing harder on the good leg), but she no longer picked up that foot straight. It broke over to the outside and then because it took more effort to break over (due to the fused pastern joint), it had an exaggerated swing--a twist that brought the foot inward (instead of outward, like a foot would normally do when breaking over to the outside).

I rode her a little that fall, checking and moving range cattle, and then to round up cattle off the range. Even though she wasn't lame, she occasionally hit her good leg with the crooked-moving foot. I've always done my own shoeing so Lynn and I experimented with corrective shoes because Fahleen was getting a sore fetlock joint from bumping it.

We finally figured out a way to shoe her that solved the problem. Lynn made a square-toed shoe and welded a dab of borium (hard-surfacing – tungston carbide) on one side of the toe of that shoe – on her off-to-the-outside breakover point. This forced her to break over the center of the toe, making her pick up the foot straight. Hence it traveled straighter in flight, without the added twisting motion, no longer hitting the opposite leg.

But she had enough other problems to keep me occupied. Her digestive tract was very sensitive, perhaps from early worm damage as a young horse. She was the first of my foals born on this ranch, the spring we moved here after Lynn and I were married. We were purchasing this place – two miles below the ranch where I grew up – along with my parent's ranch, which we now called the "upper place."

The pasture where we kept Nell and foal had been used for decades by horses of previous owners, and was probably heavily contaminated with worm eggs. Those early ranchers didn't deworm horses. Deworming was a new thing in the early 1960s and even though we tried to keep our horses dewormed, the ones at pasture probably were continually reinfected – and a foal wouldn't have as much resistance as the older horses.

Fahleen had a tendency to colic, so I was careful about her feed and water. I always limited the amount of cold water she drank at any one time while working hard, even though a horse needs to drink a lot during a days' work on the range to keep from becoming dehydrated. I learned the hard way about her extra-sensitivity after she drank from a cold stream in the mountains one hot day when I was searching for stray cattle. Even though I limited her intake to about 12 swallows at a time and spaced her drinks over several different stream crossings, she got gut cramps, wanting to lie down and roll. I had to lead her home 10 miles, wearing holes in the soles of my old boots.

I also discovered she couldn't tolerate grain. By trial and error I found that she did much better without grain, except for maybe a handful early in the morning. She stayed fit and in good condition on good hay, even during our hardest long-distance riding campaigns. Since she was in such good physical condition from all our range chores and cow checking, I rode her on several endurance rides during the early 1970s. She was less apt to colic on a long hard ride if she wasn't fed grain.

Fahleen did very well on endurance rides because of her wonderful fast trot and great stamina, but during the 60-mile Bitterroot Ride (at Hamilton, Montana), we had an accident coming into a checkpoint near the end of the ride. As we waited our turn to be checked, a young girl rode up behind us and bumped Fahleen, causing my mare to jump sideways and collide with a parked car. Her hind leg caught under the bumper, taking all the skin off the cannon bone. She finished the ride without being lame, and one of the vets helped me clip the dangling flap

Fahleen – first summer of riding.

of skin off her leg after the ride. I hosed the leg with cold water for several hours, to reduce any pain or swelling. She traveled sound the next morning at the final vet check in spite of the injury.

I suppose I was a bit rash trying to use this mare for competitive distance rides, since she didn't like strangers handling her. On our first two competitions I took her temperature myself at the vet checks, so no one would get kicked. But Fahleen's attitude got better about the check stops and by her third competition she was almost nice.

She was fun to ride on these competitions because she put her whole heart into it. Her tremendously strong trot was a joy to ride. You really haven't lived until you've ridden a trot like that for 40 miles; it's like flying! This was her kind of sport and she loved it. Forty miles in six hours, 30 miles in five hours, 20 miles in two hours, even on a badly scraped hind leg. For pure heart and willingness, and athletic endurance she was the best. She always looked good after a ride, bouncing and full of eager energy, looking like she could easily go another 40 miles and relish every minute of it.

She was a great range-riding horse for the same reason, carrying me 20 to 30 miles in an afternoon checking cattle. We covered a lot of country in a short time, to see all the cattle and check the water troughs, fences and gates. During the summer she was a six-year-old I rode her more than 2,500 miles. Part of that distance was on competitive rides, but most of it was riding range, checking our cattle.

Fahleen was an eager traveler and a willing cowhorse and we checked a lot of cows and did a lot of cattle moving. I used her to mark trail for our 40-mile Salmon River Ride, carrying big bags of spray-painted red paper plates tied behind my saddle. Most of the ride looped through our cattle range and I tied paper plates to sagebrush and trees at strategic locations to mark the trail – so no riders would get lost. We'd gather all the plates again afterward, before the cows tore them off.

The first year I used her to mark trail, she was still pretty green, and unsure about those big bags of paper plates. My kids were still too young to ride with me, so I was out there by myself. As we came around an open hillside a gust of wind hit as I dismounted to tie a plate on a small bush, and I lost the bag of plates I was holding – and red plates went flying across the mountainside. It spooked Fahleen and she took off, scattering more plates as she jumped and bucked. I called to her as I jogged after her, and she turned around and stood wide-eyed and trembling as I caught her and then started gathering up plates. We continued on with our marking route and she was ok with it, realizing that nothing was going to hurt her.

Fahleen

She was a smart mare, and a wonderful partner. But I only got to ride her a few years. The spring she was seven, we started out great, chasing cows and riding range, and competing on a 40-mile ride (placing second in the lightweight division). I planned to go on more distance rides that summer, but we never got to do them. True to form, she got into trouble because of her exuberant nature. But this time it was serious trouble and there was no way out of it. She was bucking, leaping and playing in her pen, expressing her violent displeasure because I had walked through her pen to go catch one of the yearlings and hadn't stopped to catch her. In her burst of activity she must have twisted her intestine, probably by charging full speed from one side of the pen to the other, stopping abruptly and then flinging herself off in another direction, bucking and jumping.

As soon as she stopped her violent exertions, I could see she was in pain. She immediately began to paw, and then to roll, breaking out in a sweat. I gave her an injection of smooth-muscle relaxant (the standard drug for colic, in those days) to help ease the gut cramping and relieve her pain. I walked her around, to keep her moving so she wouldn't plop down and roll. She got better for a little while and then steadily worse again, descending into pain and shock.

Our two veterinarians came out to the ranch and examined her, and suspected a twisted gut. But there was nothing they could do to correct this. She needed surgery, but they had no facility for doing equine abdominal surgery at their clinic. We would have to trailer her 140 miles to the closest equine hospital, over winding mountain roads, or 170 miles to a big town in the other direction. She was in no shape to withstand that trip.

So all we could do was treat her for shock and relieve her pain with drugs, walking her when the pain made her want to go down.

She was cold, from shock and from being drenched with sweat, so we blanketed her. As the drugs relieved the terrible pain, she didn't try so much to crash down and roll and thrash, and we were able to let her rest. There wasn't much more we could do but stay with her, comforting her, easing her pain – as hope sifted away and we began to realize she wouldn't survive this trauma. And a person does hope, always, even until near the end. There's just something inside us that won't let go until it is utterly hopeless.

She finally became too weak to stand, and my husband trudged to the house to get a gun and end her pain, but before he could return, Fahleen died with her head in my arms, cradled in my lap, trusting me. My brave, good mare, not afraid of death as humans are, but merely puzzled because her strong young body was failing. And as she nickered softly in those last moments before she went down, I had the feeling she was seeing things beyond me, something I couldn't see.

I'm too sentimental perhaps, but when Fahleen went out of my life I realized I lost a lot more than a horse. I lost a good friend. And it took a long time before I could think about her without a tear coming to my eye. The empty corral in front of the house was a constant reminder. I had to walk through it daily to go feed and water the other horses. I used to wake up in the night and look out the window to check on her, to make sure she wasn't lying too close to the fence, to make sure she was ok after a hard ride or a long day chasing cattle. I'd wake up to check on her and then realize she was no longer there.

A hundred little things reminded me of her through each day – the trails we traveled together, the wire gate on the range that she caught her foot in and tore apart (I still think of her every time I

Fahleen

Fahleen and me on the Bitterroot Ride.

open it, and we call it Fahleen's gate), the place on one trail where she spooked at a grouse flying up and nearly lost me, and so on.

Many years have passed since I lost that mare, and time has blunted the sharp pain of loss, but not the wealth of memories. She taught me a lot; she fine-tuned my horsemanship and understanding of horses, and gave me much more than I was ever able to give her. I've raised, trained and ridden a lot of good horses since Fahleen, but in so many ways she was different, and very special. Like the teacher exasperated by (and yet eventually so very proud of) the smart-aleck kid in class who ends up being head and shoulders above the rest, I feel glad that I knew her, that her life touched mine, that for awhile we traveled our paths together.

AHMAHL
Another Clown

After Fahleen was born, we bred Nell again to El Khamis, to raise a foal for my younger sister. Nell gave birth to a bay colt in April 1968. He and my first child arrived within a few days of each other. Lynn and I named our son Michael. My little sis named Nell's foal Ahmahl, spelled a little different from Amahl, Nell's first foal that we lost.

My parents and little sister spent that summer on our upper place, so Nell and her foal lived in the horse pasture above their house. In late summer my father took a church assignment in Choteau, Montana since that little church didn't have a preacher. Nell and her foal stayed here. My sister stayed with us for the rest of the summer.

My folks rented their house on our upper ranch to the pastor of the local Seventh Day Adventist church. He and his wife had a German Shepherd female that they didn't keep home. Not long after they moved in, the dog chased Nell and Ahmahl around the pasture (on July 31) and put the foal through the fence. He was three-legged lame, packing a hind leg. His hock was sliced open, clear into the joint, and was leaking joint fluid.

We called the vet, who came and examined the wound, and injected the joint. The foal's leg was so stiff and sore he could hardly walk. We kept Nell and Ahmahl in a small pen and went up there to treat his wound a couple times a day, for a week, until he could walk well enough to bring down to our place. Lynn took me up there and I rode Nell and led the foal two miles down the road to our corral.

We continued to treat his hock for more than two months, until my dad came back in October to go hunting, and take Nell and Ahmahl to Choteau on his way home. They didn't wean him until late winter, when he was nearly 10 months old. Nell actually weaned him herself. His leg was healing but the hock remained noticeably large. As he grew bigger it was not as obvious.

Ahmahl hated dogs after that. If stray dogs wandered through the pen, he chased them out – going after them with front feet and teeth. No dog was safe around him.

The summer he was a yearling, Heidi came back to the ranch to stay with us again, and brought Nell and Ahmahl. We put him overnight in the corral when they arrived, and the next morning he'd gone through the creek, under the bridge, to get out of the corral! After that he lived at pasture with our other horses.

That summer my folks moved to Boise to start a new church there (Hillview Methodist Church) and when Heidi went back to school that fall, my folks took Nell and Ahmahl to Boise when they came to get her at summer's end. She brought both horses back to the ranch again the next summer.

That fall after she was back in Boise, Heidi started training Ahmahl (by then a long two-year-old), doing a little groundwork and

Dad helped her make a few rides, leading him at first, while she was on his back. On one of those early rides he tried to jump around a little but Dad was holding him and he couldn't do much – so he reared up, and then bucked, and dumped her off.

She rode him a little, but then she bought Surrabu, a five-year-old Arabian stallion, and Surrabu became her first love. She rode Surrabu all the time and started competing on endurance rides and doing very well. Ahmahl was left on the back burner. Heidi was spending her college summers campaigning Surrabu and didn't come to the ranch anymore, so Ahmahl stayed on pasture in Boise.

The summer of 1974, after I lost Fahleen, I was short of horses to ride range on. Khamette had an old saddle sore that was hindering steady riding, and we were trying to get Nikki bred. She didn't settle when we took her to Wendy's little gray stallion, so I'd sent her to Boise to be bred to another Arabian stallion. Heidi realized she probably wouldn't be riding Ahmahl very much, and didn't really need him – since she was so busy campaigning Surrabu on endurance rides. So she decided to give me six-year-old Ahmahl as a replacement for Fahleen.

Ahmahl was still just green broke and hadn't been ridden for several years. He was fat and soft and I had to break him in gradually. He was a bit goofy, and also liked to buck a little when cantering. When he arrived, we had just two weeks to get ready for the 60-mile Bitterroot ride, and I rode him every day riding range checking cattle. Heidi had him already shod when he arrived, but he started interfering behind (hitting one hind fetlock with the opposite foot) so I reset his hind shoes and made them a bit narrower.

He wouldn't be in good enough shape to actually compete, but I wanted to go to that ride, just to finish, just to honor Fahleen's memory. Ahmahl was starting to get in shape; he'd come at a busy time when we needed to move a lot of cattle on the high range and I was riding him four or five hours a day, with a lot of trotting. He started to really stretch out and trot – with a stride like Fahleen.

The day before I took him to the Bitterroot Ride (traveling with another gal, with her horse trailer), my twin cousin Diane from California called to tell me she was coming to visit, and I invited her to come with us. She arrived that next morning in time to go with us to Hamilton. We checked Ahmahl in, and he trotted out nicely for the judges when they checked him for soundness. Margit Bessenyey (the Hungarian Countess who hosted the Bitterroot Ride) had several grandchildren there, and two of them petted Ahmahl as we waited in line.

Diane and I slept that night on the grass in front of his stall, but we didn't sleep much – we talked till the wee hours of the morning. It was great to have her there; it helped ease my grief from losing Fahleen.

The next morning we were getting ready for the ride before daylight, and all the horses hit the trail as the sun came up. Ahmahl was excited and eager, and did a fast trot for the first eight miles. Then I slowed him down because he wasn't in shape to do the whole ride at a fast trot, and made it through the first vet check ok. We had to pace ourselves on the hills, and by the noon stop I realized we wouldn't make the 40 miles on time to qualify. I took the rest of the ride more slowly. Margit's grandkids loved him. One of them ran up behind us to pat him on the rump as we came into the third check stop. I worried he might startle and kick, but he had a lot of tolerance for kids.

We finished the 40 miles that 1st day, coming in a bit late, with the drag rider. Ahmahl was starting to show signs of fatigue (dark urine). He was nervous, however, and it took a while to cool him out. He was ok, but we didn't go the second day 20 mile ride. He was a little upset when all the horses left again the next morning, but I took him out and exercised him. Even though we didn't do the second day ride, I'm glad I took him to Hamilton. Just being out on the trail that first day took some of the ache/pain out of my heart, to be able to do it in honor of Fahleen.

The day after we got home, I rode him to move range cows again, and we continued our daily cattle work. I rode him the rest of that year and he became a good cowhorse but not as agile as Nikki. He was really fast, and could outrun and head any cow, but it took him a bit longer to change direction! He was the largest and tallest of Nell's offspring and had a tremendous "engine" and plenty of power and endurance – a great front end with excellent shoulder and front legs, but his hind end was less perfect, and cow hocked. Compared to Nikki and Fahleen (both exceptionally well balanced – Nikki just on a smaller scale than Fahleen), Ahmahl looked like he was put together by a committee. But as one ride judge told me, it didn't matter what his hind end looked like; he had a great front end and the hind would follow!

He wasn't the greatest cowhorse, but we could get the job done. He wasn't afraid of anything, and this was an asset one spring day when we were moving cows and calves from the lower fields and out to the range. We calved in January and early February, and bred the cows during April and early May, so they'd all be bred before they went to the mountains. That way we could breed them to our own bulls, and breed each cow to the bull she might nick best with, and we didn't put any bulls out on the range. The other rancher who ran

Ahmahl on his first Bitterroot ride in 1974, crossing his very first bridge.

cattle out there with us for many years also calved early, and bred his cows early (he wanted his all bred to Red Angus bulls) so this worked great. We bred our cows at home and didn't have to contend with bulls on the range.

Most years we had seven different breeding pastures on the home place. That way we could choose the genetics, and not inadvertently breed a heifer to her sire, or to a bull that sired big calves at birth. We had a horned Hereford bull named Little John with the cows on the lower place and that day in mid-May we were bringing them to the corral to sort the bull off and turn the cows on the range.

Lynn and I were following the herd into a smaller pasture and I was on Ahmahl. Little John was notorious for herding his cows; he didn't want them near any other bulls, and even though we always had a buffer pasture between breeding groups, he'd herd them away from the fence. That day, he know his harem was moving into risky territory and he went charging toward the front of the herd to head them off so they couldn't go through the gate. I galloped up there on Ahmahl to head off the bull that was trying to head off the cows.

The bull was angry, and as we caught up with him to chase him away from the gate he was blocking, the bull took a swipe at us with his horns. Ahmahl never faltered; he simply reared up and pawed with his front feet, striking the bull in the head. That startled Little John; he wasn't expecting to be hit in the face with shod hooves, and he backed off. Ahmahl and I held off the bull so the cows could funnel through the gate. I've had some good cowhorses that wouldn't back down from a job and really put their heart in it, but I'd never had any put their front feet into it, too!

Ahmahl was a character, and like his sister Fahleen was a real clown with a lively sense of humor. He was always doing little tricks to try to get the best of a person. If I was working with him on the ground, grooming, saddling, getting ready to bridle him, etc., he might nonchalantly step on my foot and then turn around and look at me as if to say, oh, did I do that? After he casually clomped down and caught both boot toes under his foot, I started reacting to his every little hint of movement or weight shift by moving my feet out of harm's way.

To backtrack a little and elaborate on his wicked sense of humor – the second year I had him, he bucked me off three times. The first time was on one of the first rides after his winter vacation, as I was riding down our snowy road with big drifts on each side. When we were about half a mile from home, a car was coming up the road, and I didn't want to ride off the road into the drift. I galloped Ahmahl down to the jeep road turnoff, to get off the main road and out of the way before the car got to us.

The gallop turned into a buck as we headed onto the jeep road and he bucked down the hill and lost me after about the fourth buck. He was a strong and agile bucker and knew he could get rid of a rider (after having dumped my sister when she was starting him under saddle). He gleefully left me sitting in the snow and galloped home. I picked myself up out of the snowdrift and jogged home after him.

Later that spring I was moving cows along Baker Creek, moving them from the low range to the middle range pasture. Ahmahl and I were on the rim of a little canyon, going through some brush and rocks to follow part of the herd. He suddenly bucked, out of the blue. I wasn't prepared for a buck, so he easily lost me and ran across the draw, over the hill and home. I had to jog more than a mile that time, and he was back in the barnyard happily munching grass when I caught up with him.

I rode him nearly every day checking range cattle through the next month and he never tried to buck. In July I rode him on the Salmon River 40-mile ride and placed second in the lightweight division.

Beth Yost was working for us, and she and I planned to go to several more Rocky Mountain Conference rides that summer, in Montana. Beth was the little sister of the guy my college roommate married, and loved horses. She'd always wanted to be on a ranch, so she came to work for us the summer of 1975, with her horse trailer and Morgan gelding, and ended up staying several years, helping with haying, range riding, etc. We took our two horses to conference rides in 1975 and 1976.

After the Salmon Ride in 1975 Ahmahl scraped his back, rolling on a rock in his pen, and I gave him 10 days off to let it heal enough that my saddle wouldn't open up the scab. During that time I used Khamette or Nikki to check cows. The first ride after his layoff, I made a fast six-hour loop over the range checking cows, and started home through the middle range pasture, down a mountain trail. I came across another group of cows and checked them off in my cow book (always carried in my hip pocket). After marking off all those cows and calves, I tucked the little notebook back in my pocket, riding on a loose rein, and he took that opportunity to buck, knowing I wasn't prepared to stop him. As I catapulted up into the air all I had time to do was yell his name!

Since we were going downhill on a steep trail, it was a long way to the ground after he pitched me over his head. I did a forward roll when I hit, landing between two big rocks. My guardian angel was on duty because my only injuries were a cut ear and a bruised, sprained shoulder. Ahmahl ran off a little ways, then stopped. I'm glad he didn't try to run home that time, because we were several miles from home and my shoulder hurt pretty badly. He was smart. He knew he couldn't run all the way home because there was a gate we had to go through, about a mile farther down the mountain. So I sweet-talked him and he stopped to graze, and let me walk up and catch him, all innocent-like as if he'd done nothing wrong at all.

I managed to get on okay on the uphill side, but had trouble getting through the tight wire gate a mile farther down the creek and shutting it again with just one good arm, and a challenge mounting him again, using one arm. But he seemed to know I needed him to be a good boy (he didn't mean to do me harm; the bucking was fun and games). He stood still and was patient as I struggled to get on.

My arm was sore for a while but it didn't keep me from riding every day. On the next few rides Beth was with me and she opened

*Ahmal and me (right) in 1976 on the Bitterroot Ride,
where he won first place in the lightweight division.*

and shut the range gates until my arm was less painful. She and I did some of the other rides on the conference later that summer, and Ahmahl placed first on the 40-mile Squaw Peak Ride and sixth on the 60-mile Bitterroot Ride. He never bucked me off again – I always rode him like a green horse after that, prepared for anything, never slopping along with loose reins, and he knew it was pointless to try. He knew that I knew that he knew, and we got along just fine.

The next spring – 1976 – we were moving cattle on our low range pasture and he trotted through some sharp rocks to head a wayward cow and stone bruised a front foot. He was lame several days. The bruise abscessed and I had to open up his sole and drain and soak it. The bruise healed, but he had a big hole in his sole that took all summer to fill in. It was such a big hole, I kept his foot wrapped so he wouldn't get dirt and gravel in it.

I considered shoeing him with hoof pads, but thought it wouldn't give enough protection if we were trotting through rocks. The pads are flexible and a sharp rock could still poke into that big hole and make him sore. I didn't want to risk it, so I didn't ride him on the Salmon River Ride, just helped put it on. I talked to Doc Hatfield, one of the ride vets and a good friend, and asked his advice. He suggested we weld a metal plate on his shoe, to cover the hole in his sole. This would give more protection than a hoof pad.

Lynn and I created a special shoe for Ahmahl. The hole was just an inch behind the toe, a little to one side, so Lynn cut a piece of metal the proper size and welded it to the shoe, to cover that hole. I put the shoe on, and started riding Ahmahl again. He did fine after that, chasing cows in the rocks.

When it came time to reset his shoes, Lynn created another "armor plated" shoe for the other front foot, to keep it from stone bruising (since Ahmahl had flat feet) and balance his stride – so he'd have even weight on both fronts. He welded hard-surfacing material ("borium" – tungsten carbide – used on oil-drilling bits) onto both shoes so they wouldn't wear out. This material is harder than diamonds and keeps the shoe from wearing away on rocks. We could use those same shoes the rest of the summer and wouldn't have to keep making new ones with metal plating welded on them.

With his special shoes, Ahmahl happily trotted and galloped through even the rockiest terrain with no fear of hurting his feet, chasing cows and competing on three more rides that year. He got first place on the Big Sky Ride, fourth place at Kalispell, first place on the Bitterroot Ride.

We had an interesting episode with Ahmahl when we got ready to leave for the Squaw Peak ride that summer. We loaded Beth's horse, then I started to lead Ahmahl in and he refused! He'd ridden thousands of miles in trailers (to Montana with his mom when he was a foal, back and forth between the ranch and Boise when Heidi brought him and Nell with her for the summers, and then all our trail ride competitions), yet that day he decided he's not going in a trailer! It took an hour of encouragement – and finally some coercion – to convince him to go in. Then three days later when we finished that ride event and were ready to come home, he again refused to get in the trailer. One of our friends who was there from Salmon gave us a little help, spanking Ahmahl on the rump with his lariat, and Ahmahl jumped right in. He never again refused to go in a trailer, and I think he was just trying us out to see if we really meant it.

The next competitive ride was near Kalispell, Montana. It was a cool drizzly day when we started the ride, but fairly warm, so we didn't put on our coats. We were soaked before noon, and the trail was muddy. We put on our coats for the rest of the ride but we were already wet, and cold. It rained harder as the day progressed, and the trail got boggy. Those of us at the front of the pack had better footing than the riders farther back because the trail was churned up by dozens of horses' feet by then.

Partway through the second half of the ride, Beth and I realized we were running late and would have to go faster to finish on time to qualify. We'd been trotting, but the slippery trail had probably slowed our horses more than we realized. So we hurried. I was glad Ahmahl was surefooted because we were flying at an extended trot over a very muddy trail. That's when I found out what a truly fast extended trot he could do! His trot was much too fast to post; I simply stood in my stirrups. My raw knees were painful – rubbed raw by wet jeans on the 40-mile ride!

HORSE TALES

For the last two miles we were going full out, to make it on time. Beth's gangly Morgan gelding was a trotter; he shifted gears, dropped down about a foot in height and did a racing trot like a Standardbred, and Ahmahl had to gallop to keep up with him. Beth's knees were as raw as mine by that time, and we were wet, cold and miserable! We finished the ride on time, but many riders did not. After we got our horses checked in, cooled out and taken care of, we huddled in the camper shell on her pickup, in our sleeping bags – after taking off our soaked clothes – trying to get warm. Ahmahl's range riding conditioning paid off on that ride; he placed first in the lightweight division.

Those were good rides, good times, good memories, but that was the last year we traveled to other rides. After that, life was just too busy. Also, I wasn't riding Ahmahl as regularly. The next summer, 1977, I was training Nikkolis and Khamir, who were four-year-olds. Ahmahl wasn't the kind of horse you could just turn out in a pasture or pen and just ride him once in a while. It took steady, regular riding to keep him honest.

By that time my sister Heidi had graduated from college, starting in vet school and short of money – and she knew a fellow who was looking for a good endurance horse. I gave Ahmahl back to Heidi, to sell to that person. Ahmahl was perfect for that rider, who was looking for a big horse with a big heart and a lot of endurance. His new owner was a big man who felt funny riding a little Arab. On his try-out ride on Ahmahl, they galloped to the top of a steep mountain and Ahmahl took a couple deep breaths and was ready to go again. In his new career as an endurance horse, the goofy gelding would be traveling enough miles to keep him happy and honest, so I trust they got along fine.

SURROCCO
A Challenge

After unsuccessfully trying to get another foal from Nell (we bred her to our leased stallion Sur Amir, in 1972, but she didn't settle), we bred her one more time, in 1973, when she was 20. This time we bred her to my little sister's Arabian stallion Surrabu, and she foaled a nice bay colt on May 12, 1974. I named him Surrocco. He was the last of Nell's children. Realizing that we probably would never get another foal from her, I didn't geld him, thinking I might to use him to sire a few more good ranch horses from that line. He was well built, athletic, and smart – too smart. Training him proved to be a challenge.

From the time he was a foal, he liked to play games, just to see if he could get the best of me. He kept me on my toes to keep one jump ahead of him so I was in control. I did a lot of groundwork with him, to keep handling him regularly and keep the rapport (and remind him that I was team leader). I didn't want to start riding him at a young age because he had so much fire and spirit that he would have been bored doing kindergarten things for very long; he needed to go lots of miles to burn off some of that exuberant energy, and I wanted him to be physically mature enough to go the necessary miles. I planned to start him under saddle the summer he was a three-year-old.

We generally train our horses on the job, riding range, chasing cows, because they learn a lot more, a lot quicker, that way, and don't get bored doing repeated maneuvers. Our Anglo-Arabs always wanted a job to do and enjoyed a good job – something to occupy their minds and employ all that athletic energy. The spring of his three-year-old year I tried to take time to lead him nearly every day, because he was becoming more aggressive, bold and headstrong, and quite full of himself as a young stallion. I began using a chain over his nose because he needed more reminder that I was the one leading him instead of him leading me.

One day in early summer I went to catch him and he came charging up to greet me at the gate. One of the mares in the adjacent pen was in heat, and Surrocco had been running along the fence in frustration. She was standing right by the gate, on her side of the fence, when I went to catch him. He bumped the electric wire and shocked himself as he came charging up to me. That upset him and he ran off.

When he came back and I started to catch him, he grabbed me by the back of the neck and picked me up with his teeth. I yelled and he let go. I dropped to the ground and ducked under the electric wires into the next pen. He was angry and frustrated and took out that frustration on me. I realized we had to geld him. He had potential to be a great cow horse and I didn't want to fight with an aggressive stallion. I made an appointment with our vet to do the surgery.

I didn't catch him again till that day, and tried to forget about his biting me. My neck was bruised and sore but nothing serious. We planned to geld him in our grassy back yard. A few minutes ahead of when the vet was to arrive, I caught Surrocco (the mare was no longer in heat, in the next pen, which made things easier) and let him graze in the yard. I sat on a cinder block, hanging onto the end of his rope, letting him graze, trying to keep everything peaceful and non-confrontational. He kept pulling at the rope, wanting to graze farther away, and I kept him grazing in a circle around me.

Restraint by the rope made him mad. Suddenly he raised his head, with a strange look in his eyes, and lunged. As I stood up to defend myself he hit me in the chest with his teeth, knocking me down. I scrambled to my feet and still had the rope in my hands as I ran toward the little gate with him coming after me. I went outside the yard and slammed the gate behind me, holding the rope over the fence. Lynn came running when he heard me yell, and grabbed the rope. He tied up Surrocco while I went to the house to get ice (and stuffed an ice pack under my bra) to halt the swelling over the broken ribs. The vet arrived and we gelded Surrocco there in the back yard.

He was still aggressive, but a little more subdued after the surgery. Lynn helped me with the daily aftercare, using a fly-repellent on his incisions and making sure they were open and draining. I longed him for exercise to help reduce swelling. Then I started saddling and mounting him, but he was still angry. Lynn had to hold him for me as I got on, because he tried to rush backward. With his attitude, this wasn't working. I decided to give him time to get all the testosterone out of his system, and start over later. My ribs hurt all summer. It was painful to laugh, cough or sneeze, and I had to be careful riding range and chasing cows. I didn't start riding Surroco till he was a five-year old. We had to rebuild our relationship and learn to trust each other again – and it took a while. He was still headstrong and feisty, trying to avoid my getting on him, but we worked through our distrust.

After a couple of rides in the calving pen, I decided to head over

161

our low range to give him more to look at and think about. My first ride over the hills, Lynn hiked with me to make sure things would be okay. Surrocco did fine, so I began making longer rides, with our nine-year-old daughter Andrea riding with me on Brownie. By that time she was an excellent rider and seasoned range-rider-cowgirl.

Surrocco never bucked me off. The only time he ever lost me (that I didn't bail off – but that's another story) was about the second ride across the low range, when a grouse flew up in his face. He whirled – more than 180 degrees – and slung me out of the saddle. I landed on my feet, still holding the reins, standing in front of him – with one boot gone and just a sock on. I'm glad I didn't land on a cactus! The force of his spin (as my foot twisted out of the stirrup) pulled my boot off and it sailed over the bushes. Andrea found my boot and brought it back to me. I rebooted, remounted, and we continued on our way. From then on we've called that spot in the trail "lost boot alley."

By the end of that riding season he'd become dependable. We'd gone lots of hard miles, checked a lot of gates and fences and chased a lot of cows. He was always thinking, calculating, always level-headed in spite of his high spirits. He did fine with other horses along, or by himself. Even though he was goofy and liked to act spooky, he never panicked. Except once.

Andrea and I were riding Brownie and Surrocco down Withington Creek after checking range cows and came around a bend where there was a little meadow. Someone had camped there, with a big piece of plastic – maybe a makeshift tent. That wasn't a big deal, but a young boy who was sitting beside it crawled under the plastic to hide from us and here's this wiggly big plastic thing making strange noises! Our horses freaked out, confronting this thing from outer space. They whirled and bolted up the mountainside, scrambling in the bad

I had to start using a nose chain when exercising young Surrocco.

footing. We yelled at the kid to come out – so the horses could see that it was just a human. Finally the kid came out from under the plastic and we got past this crazy roadblock.

Usually, however, nothing bothered him. One time during a rainstorm – when he was still very green--I went through a pole gate and opened it from horseback. I was riding through and Surrocco went too close to the gatepost and caught my stirrup on the wire loop. Rather than panic and tear up my saddle, he stopped, and let me maneuver things around and get unhooked.

Another time, early in his riding career, we came home from a long ride and I started to take my saddle off after I loosened my cinch, and didn't realize it wasn't completely unhooked. The saddle came sideways and ended up under his belly and he jumped backward. I thought, "Oh shit! Here's a big wreck!" But he stopped dead still and waited for me to extricate him.

HORSE TALES

On the range I could get off, put the reins over the saddle horn, and climb through a fence to chase a calf on the wrong side (to get it moving in the direction of a gate or spot in the fence where I could get it back to the proper side), and he'd walk along, following on his side.

I could ride him in thick brush after a cow and he'd worm his way through the branches and over logs and never get upset or excited, and go as slow as necessary for me to duck through (if I was on him) or lead him. The only time we got too jungled up was when we were following cows through brush and down trees along a fence and I had to try to turn him to go after some other cows. He tried to turn in the thick brush and ended up backing up a few steps – and hit some logs with his hind legs, tripping him. He reared up, and I feared he might lose his balance and go over backward in that pile of logs. I bailed off, to make sure I wouldn't end up underneath him. He scrambled and got his bearings again, and we continued moving the cows.

Of all my horses, he had the highest pain tolerance. Though he was flatfooted, he clambered through the rockiest terrain chasing cows without getting tender. Dings and bumps that might slow down most horses never phased him. One time we were moving cows up through a creek bottom where there down trees and broken branches and he ran a sharp stick into his coronary band. He limped for a moment, and I looked down and saw the stick jammed in above his hoof, so I got off and tried to pull it out. I got most of it, but it broke off inside. He wasn't lame anymore so I continued the cattle drive.

Five or six hours later, after we got home, Lynn used needle-nosed pliers and pulled more wood out of the hole above his hoof. I soaked his foot in warm water and Epsom salts daily for a few days, but he was never lame and I kept riding him. Two weeks later, on another cattle drive, I felt him walking a little funny and looked down and saw more wood working out of that hole! I got off and was able to pull it on out. Probably the soaking, and all the riding and exercise, helped it work out. After those fragments came out, the puncture healed.

His worst habit was unpredictable tying. Sometimes he'd set back, for no reason. One time he set back when he was tied and saddled, waiting while Andrea and I were in the corral sorting cattle we were taking to the range. The rope broke and he went over backward. I was afraid he'd smashed my saddle. But all he smashed was the stirrup. I had to steal a stirrup off another saddle to ride that day.

Another time he set back when I tied him to fix a water trough on the range. He pulled the knot so tight around the tree I couldn't get it loose. Our halter ropes were braided into the halters, not snapped, so I was afraid I'd have to cut the rope to get him loose, but finally used a nail out of an old pole by the trough to pick at the knot.

Surrocco had tremendous endurance, even more than Nell's other children (and they were darn tough!). I could use him hard – trotting and galloping--day after day, sometimes nine or 10 hours a day or longer during our roundups gathering cows, and never wear him out. The only time he got a little tired was the day Andrea and I moved cattle out of the forks of Withington Creek during a fall roundup and then had to chase part of them some more, for several hours. This was only about the fourth time I'd ridden him all year; he'd had time off because of a sore back. I had to ride Surrocco that day for some reason that I can no longer recall.

Our range neighbors (Kosslers) helped gather cows out of the forks and bring them over the ridge into the Baker Creek drainage. By then it was late in the day (we'd already ridden nine hours), so they planned to come back the next day to help sort cattle in upper Baker Creek – and take their cows home through the middle range pasture while we put ours into our half-section of private pasture (the "320").

Kosslers headed home, and Andrea and I, riding Surrocco and Katy, came down the other ridge on our way home, to let in our cows that were already down in the fence corner by our 320. We put them into our place and were about to start home, when we saw dozens of cattle pouring down the ridge above us. Instead of easing the herd down off the divide between Withington Creek and Baker Creek on their way home, Kosslers had just left them there on top. Soon after Kosslers left, cattle started drifting down the wrong ridge and instead of going into Baker Creek they poured down toward our fence corner.

If they came down in there, it would be a harder job to get Kossler's cattle out the next morning; those cattle would have to climb a half mile up the steep mountain to go up and around our fence before they could head toward the middle range and home. Andrea and I galloped back up the hill to head them off and send them toward Baker Creek, where it would be easier for Kosslers to pick them up the next day. We were also afraid they might come through the fence to get to water if we let them come on down into that lower corner.

Our horses had already had a full day's work, but if we could get those cattle turned it would save a lot of work the next day and be easier on the cows. Andrea and I galloped back and forth, trying to head them all as they poured down the hill. They were fanned out over the hillside about a quarter mile so we were having a tough time getting them turned before they got below our upper fence corner.

We managed to get them all halted in their downhill onslaught, and got them drifting around the top of our fence, toward Baker Creek, but our horses had to work at speed nonstop for 2 hours. Toward the end, Katy was worn out and I was having to do most of the runs back and forth, and actually had to urge Surrocco a little

Surrocco inspects Beth's trailer.

because he was tired. That's the only time I ever came close to the bottom of his reserve endurance.

He went a lot of hard miles for me, uphill and down. Even in old age he stayed sound and never went lame, but his back got stiff. He had trouble going down steep hills and was more comfortable jogging downhill than walking. No matter how steep or how bad the footing, we managed ok if he could jog; it seemed to be easier on his back.

The last year of his life, his teeth were bad, he was a bit thin, and he was slow to shed off after winter. During his final summer, he had trouble keeping his weight, so that fall we put him down. It was the end of an era; he was the last of Nell's children. We've had many good ranch horses over the years, but Nell's half-Arab offspring were the best.

BROWNIE
The Substitute Who Made Good

When our children were very young we wanted to raise a horse for each of them to ride as they grew up. In 1972 we bred my half-Arab mare Khamette and Lynn's Quarter Horse mare Bambi to an Arabian stallion we'd leased for that summer, in hopes of producing foals for our kids. We also bred my good Anglo-Arab mare, Nikki (my best cowhorse) to raise another good cowhorse. Nikki was more high-strung than the other two mares and we didn't think a foal from her would be mellow enough for a child. The other two mares might be perfect mamas to raise "kid" horses.

Khamette was 13 – a very dependable ranch horse that I'd raised and trained when I was a teenager. Bambi was a nice Quarter Horse mare my husband bought as a five-year-old in 1966, the year we were married. Both mares had wonderful dispositions and our children (ages four and two, in 1972) had already been riding those two gentle mares.

Best-laid plans do not always come to fruition. Nikki had a good bay colt named Nikkolis. Khamette had a chestnut filly, named Khamir – destined to become our three-year-old daughter Andrea's first horse of her own. Bambi didn't do so well. About a month before she was due to foal, I noticed that her udder was starting to develop. I didn't think she would foal for a while, however, because our other mares in the past had "bagged up" for several days or even weeks before foaling. Mares are notorious for foaling a few weeks early or late; they are not as predictable as cattle. They usually make some sign that they are about to foal, however – but not always, as Bambi demonstrated.

The very next day, when I went out in the early morning to do my feeding chores, I noticed Bambi wandering around her pen, acting uncomfortable. I looked more closely and saw two tiny feet protruding from her vulva. She was foaling! But the feet were upside down – which meant the foal was coming backward.

I rushed back in the house and told Lynn, and we quickly went into action. I caught the mare and held her, with obstetrical chains ready, as Lynn carefully felt inside her. A backward delivery generally needs assistance; otherwise the foal is not born quickly enough to survive. Its head is still inside the mare when the cord pinches off.

What Lynn discovered was more serious than the backward presentation. The foal's front legs were coming into the birth canal; the foal was doubled up with all four feet coming at once. It could never be born in this position. He tried to push the foal back into the uterus where there was more room to straighten it out, but couldn't.

I ran to call the vet. Our regular vet was busy with another case, and sent his young assistant. The young vet had never dealt with a situation like this, and could not straighten the foal. It was dead by that time, and the vet opted to cut up the fetus so he could bring the pieces out through the birth canal. He finally got that accomplished, and then discovered that Bambi had a rip in her uterus. This is very serious, but one of our vets had recently saved a mare with this condition, sewing the tear back together. The young vet was not willing to try this difficult procedure however, and since the mare had no other chance to survive, he put her to sleep. Thus in one tragic morning we lost not only our dream for young Michael's first horse, but also lost Lynn's good mare.

Later that year, however, we were able to acquire a substitute horse for our son. We met a young couple, new to our valley, living on a small acreage the other side of town, raising Appaloosa horses. The McBrides had a young daughter Michael's age and often came to visit. That fall we had a big yearling steer we planned to butcher, and since this young family needed meat, we gave them half. They offered to make us a trade – half a beef for a yearling colt.

The colt they wanted to give us was from their registered Appaloosa herd, but he had no "color." He was plain brown, with no spots, and therefore wasn't worth much as an Appaloosa. If he'd been a filly, they might have kept him as a broodmare, in hopes to produce foals with spots, but in their eyes he would be worthless as a gelding.

We went to their place to look at the colt, and though he was very plain looking (big feet and a big head) and skinny, he seemed gentle. He was in a grazed-down pasture with other horses, and was very placid, letting us catch and pet him. We thought he might make a good "first horse" for our son, and made the trade. We couldn't afford to buy a horse so trading half a beef for a young horse seemed like a logical solution. Our son Michael named him Brownie.

We brought Brownie home and he lived in a pen by our old

Brownie

Andrea working cattle in the corral on Brownie.

barn, where we could feed him separate from the other horses – to be sure he'd get enough food. We gelded him and dewormed him. After deworming and adequate feed, he quickly gained weight and attitude! We discovered he was not as "gentle" as we thought; he was just so run down from being wormy and malnourished that he didn't have the strength or desire to show his sassy, independent nature. After a few months at our place he was a totally different horse. Even after we gelded him, he continued to "blossom" in spunk and spirit and stubborn independence, and his true colors began to show.

Literally. When he shed his winter coat the next spring at the beginning of his two-year-old year, he was no longer solid-colored dull brown, but had flecks of white in his coat. The next few years, he sported more white hairs. He never had a spectacular

Appaloosa "blanket" with spots, but developed an interesting mottling of white hairs on parts of his body, and finally showed his Appaloosa heritage.

I started riding him a little that summer, to train him as thoroughly as possible and have him dependable and trustworthy for our young son. Brownie was hard-headed but smart, and by the time he was three I was able to ride him out on the range to check cattle.

He never grew very big, which made him perfect for the kids, and he wasn't built like a modern Appaloosa (highly influenced by Quarter Horse breeding, with large muscles, wide chest, and small feet). Brownie was more like the old Indian horses--plain and homely, with a narrow chest and body and big feet. Like the Indian ponies, he was also surefooted and had a lot of endurance. He became a good ranch horse and carried both kids many miles. He was good at chasing cows in rugged terrain. Our kids have good memories of many wild rides and heroic cow chases on Brownie. He was one of the most surefooted horses we had, for running full speed downhill in bad terrain.

After I'd ridden Brownie two summers and had him well trained, our young son Michael (age eight by then) started riding him. Brownie was very flat-footed and I had to shoe his front feet with hoof pads, to protect them from bruising.

Brownie adapted quickly to being a "kid" horse and was dependable, though lazy. He realized he didn't have to work much, packing a child around. When Michael rode with us to check cattle, Brownie might lag behind, or try to stop and eat grass. He didn't want to climb steep hills, and we'd look back and see Michael struggling to get Brownie to go up the hill. Andrea, six years old, had the same problem with Khamette. I was still training Andrea's young mare, Khamir, and Andrea was riding old Khamette until she could ride her feisty young mare. Andrea's short legs didn't reach below the saddle pad, and the mare could hardly feel her kicking. So we bought each child a riding crop – so they could tap their mounts on the rump to encourage them to go.

Brownie was usually very trustworthy, taking good care of his young rider. If Michael had to get off to open a gate, Brownie waited patiently, even if Michael didn't keep hold of the reins. He wasn't as patient with an adult rider. If you didn't keep hold of him, he'd take off and go home, leaving you stranded.

Brownie never bucked with either of the children when they were small, but he did lose Michael a couple of times. First was when we were heading across our low range to go move cattle. Velma Ravndal (whose horses we were boarding, after Jerry died and she sold their ranch and broodmares) and Beth Yost (working for us that summer) were both riding with us. I was in the lead, riding Ahmahl, who was still green.

The trail went through a gully, and sometimes horses tried to jump it. We'd all crossed the gully except Michael and Brownie. I heard a shriek and looked back, and Michael was sitting on the ground – and Brownie was galloping back down the trail toward home. Brownie had jumped the gully instead of walking nicely through it, and Michael had tumbled off. Brownie decided to go home instead of following the other horses.

He had a head start, but after making sure Michael was ok, I took off after him. It took nearly a mile to catch up with him, pass him, and grab his reins. Then came the challenge of leading him back to his young rider. Ahmahl had never led another horse before, and Brownie had never been led from another horse, so they both had a learning experience. We eventually got back to the group, and continued our range ride.

Brownie lost his young rider one other time, when we were all galloping over a mountain to "save" a young doe that was cornered by coyotes on a rocky outcropping. We heard the deer screaming and hurried around the mountain – just in time to chase the coyotes away. But while galloping through the rocks and sagebrush, Brownie stepped in a hole and stumbled, tossing Michael off over his head. The child was unhurt, and since Brownie stopped for him that time, he quickly climbed back on and caught up with us.

Michael became an excellent rider, and never fell off Brownie again. He learned how to anticipate gully-jumping, and leaned forward to ride over the jump and keep from being left behind. But during one wild cow chase when he and Brownie had to jump a deep gully to head off a wayward cow, Michael leaned too far forward over Brownie's neck and caught his ribcage on the saddle horn. When Brownie landed and Michael snapped back into position, it tore his lower ribs loose from his breastbone. He was in terrible pain, but managed to finish the ride – and we took him to the doctor when we got home. The doctor sent us to a specialist because he feared surgery would be needed, but the specialist said the ribs would eventually heal, which they did.

During the 1970s Lynn and I helped put on the annual 40-mile Salmon River Ride that went through our range. The kids and I marked trail each year, tying red-painted paper plates to trees and sagebrush along the route, and picked them up after the ride. When Michael was 10, he was finally old enough to compete on these rides, and had his heart set on riding Brownie. He stayed with the other riders the night before the ride, at the camp area on

Young Michael enjoying a quiet moment with his horse.

the upper end of our ranch. My dad brought his horse Jon Boy from Boise, and Michael was staying with him. Dad's horse and Brownie were tied to trees by their tent.

But at daylight Brownie was gone! He'd untied himself and tried to come home. He'd come partway down the back side of our place, but got tangled in an old wire fence, and cut his shoulder. He bled profusely, and his leg was stiff and swollen.

Michael was in tears. His horse was seriously hurt, and he would not be able to compete on the ride. We brought Brownie home in Dad's trailer and grabbed old Khamette out of her pasture, and took her to the camp. Michael rode her on the competitive ride instead of Brownie.

Fortunately the wounds were just in muscle tissue; no tendons were cut. He healed, and by summer's end Michael could ride him a little. He was completely healed by the next spring and Michael rode him on the competitive ride that year.

As time went on, Brownie got a lot of use, being ridden by both kids. When Michael was helping Lynn with haying, Andrea used Brownie as a spare horse, to give her own mare an occasional rest. She and I rode nearly every day, putting in long hours checking cattle, fences and gates, fixing water troughs, moving cattle. Brownie proved to be tough and agile, able to endure long days chasing cows.

One of the wildest chases wasn't a cow roundup, however, but to catch a wild mustang. Andrea was riding Brownie the day she went with me to accompany our range neighbor Galen Kossler and a young BLM employee who wanted to ride over our range and map the different types of soils and vegetation. The BLM employee (whom we'll call John) was riding a BLM mustang he'd adopted and was starting to train. The mare was still unpredictable, and very skittish as the young man took her out of his trailer and tried to get on her. As we started out over the mountains, Galen joked about needing a butterfly net to catch him if he got bucked off.

We traveled through our middle pasture and John was taking notes, listing plants that were representative of certain soil types. He had a clipboard, charts and other papers in his saddlebags. We'd been at this project several hours, showing him the range, and his mare had behaved fairly well. Then she spooked as we came around a trail high on a windy ridge. She exploded into bucking. John lost his clipboard and tried valiantly to ride it out, but went off over her head. The mare took off at a dead run through the rocks and timber. John picked himself up and said, "She'll be a hard one to catch!"

I stayed at the scene to make sure John was ok, and helped gather up his clipboard and papers that were strung over the hill. Andrea and Galen took off after the departed mustang. Galen was on a big Quarter Horse/Thoroughbred that he was very proud of, and was sure he could catch up with the mustang (and took off well ahead of Andrea), but Andrea – with her cow-savvy experience-- charged down through the timber below the mare, to head her off. Brownie was used to chasing cows in this kind of terrain and he got below the mare, running neck and neck with her around the mountain. They ran about a quarter mile and Andrea was able to grab the rope.

She was able to hang onto the mare until Galen caught up, and then he grabbed the rope. But he didn't have time to take a dally around his saddle horn and she pulled away from him and took off again. Andrea and Brownie chased her down again, running her into a big patch of fir trees, which slowed her down, and Andrea was able to grab the trailing rope again. This time Galen got the rope dallied, about three wraps around the horn, and he and his big strong horse were able to drag the mustang back to John. Andrea was very proud of her scrawny little sure-footed cowhorse that day, and John was very relieved that he didn't have to walk home!

NIKKOLIS
The Horse with the Greatest Imagination

W e've had many horses over the years, each with a very different personality. The one with the most fertile imagination was Nikkolis, the son of my best cowhorse, Nikki. We bred Nikki in 1972, to an Arabian stallion named Sur Amir that we kept on the ranch that year. Nikki was 10 years old at that time, and I was hoping to get a foal that would be a really good cowhorse, like she was.

Her foal, Nikkolis, was born April 26, 1973. He grew up taller than his sire or his dam; he threw back to the Thoroughbred ancestry. But in spite of his long legs, he was very agile, nearly as agile as his mama, and he served me well as a good cowhorse.

Nikkolis is long gone now, but he left us with interesting memories. He was a nervous, ambitious character, and though he mellowed in old age, he always had the jaunty step and sprightly attitude of a young colt − all fired up to meet the next challenge around the bend in the trail. He was always in a hurry and it took several years of patient work and lots of miles to get him to relax enough to walk instead of wanting to trot or prance. We used to joke about his attempts to live up to his racehorse heritage; his great-great-great-grandsire Pillory won the Preakness and the Belmont in 1922 but wasn't entered in the Kentucky Derby. Maybe Nikkolis was trying to make up for that one.

He was never lazy, and a great horse to ride if a person had many miles to go, in a hurry. He was the horse we chose if we had to check gates at the far corner of our range where a jeep road went through, to make sure these weren't left open for the cows to find and drift into the wrong range.

He could outrun any cow, and was agile enough to outmaneuver devious bovines, but there was one time we had a wreck (me, not him) because he was getting stiff in his old age and didn't want to maneuver quite as fluidly as he did in his youth. Andrea and I were bringing an open cow down off the range to sell, and she didn't want to come. We got her into our 320-acre mountain pasture and she ran as fast as she could toward the creek bottom to ditch out in the trees. Nikkolis and I were heading her off – and beat her to the trees – but as we weaved through the outlying aspens at full-out gallop, he curved just enough to miss a tree, but not enough for my knee to miss it. My left knee crashed flat-smash against an aspen tree at about 30 mph.

Wow! That hurt! We got the cow, and took her on down to the ranch (about three miles) but my knee was starting to swell. I put ice on it when we got home, kept an ice pack strapped on the rest of the day, slept with an ice pack, rode all the next day (because we had to gather cattle to move to the high range) with ice wrapped around my knee (and that leg hanging because it wouldn't bend to put my foot in the stirrup) and *then* went to the doctor the next day. He took an x-ray and was amazed the kneecap wasn't broken. Just a bunch of blood under the kneecap. He estimated about 2 liters of fluid in the swelling--from broken blood vessels--and my leg turned black clear down to my foot. The leg was colorful all summer and I had to work at getting full motion back in the knee, but at least I didn't have to ride range in a cast!

Even in old age, Nikkolis was always eager to go-go-go, but also had the sort of personality that inspired the saying, "Afraid of his own shadow." Actually he was much more imaginative than that. He didn't spook at his own shadow, but rather at much more terrifying visions. I never quite figured out how his mind worked, but riding him was never boring. It was guaranteed to keep you awake – very much awake. He was my best cowhorse for more than a dozen years (after his mother passed on at age 25 – he took her place very nicely), and he was wonderful to ride if I had to chase cattle through difficult terrain. He was fleet and agile and put his whole heart and soul into outrunning and outmaneuvering a wayward cow, over logs and bogs or crashing through the brush if necessary, and we always got the cow. But if we didn't need to run after an uncooperative critter – and his mind wasn't totally occupied by outsmarting and outmaneuvering a wily cow – he'd think up all kinds of interesting things to spook at.

He was such an honest horse that he'd never dream of doing anything really naughty like bucking; he only bucked on one occasion and only because he was scared, not naughty. That was the day Lynn was riding him, to babysit a green filly ("Rubbie") I was starting under saddle. I'd done kindergarten rides on her in the barnyard and we were venturing into the big wide world on our low range. Lynn came along on Nikkolis during those early

Nikkolis spooking at an imaginary thin bear hiding behind a tree.

rides, to give Rubbie confidence when encountering new things.

We did fine until about the third ride when we decided to go farther and cross Baker Creek — a little stream that comes down through that pasture. We were riding along the old jeep road, and it crossed the stream. Rubbie didn't think that was such a great idea. She'd grown up in a small pasture with no streams — and her idea about getting her feet wet only extended to walking through irrigation water.

Nikkolis crossed the stream first, to show her it was no big deal. To her it *was* a big deal. She didn't want to follow Nikkolis. No way. No how. I untied the halter rope that I'd tied to the saddle horn, and handed it to Lynn, to lead her through. Nope. In her early lessons we hadn't ponied her from another horse and she balked. So Lynn got off his horse and led her across the stream on foot. That worked.

The filly was broke to lead and she came across as he led her.

That was fine and dandy, but when Lynn got back on Nikkolis he forgot to check his cinch. It was a bit loose and the saddle turned as he got on – just enough to be a bit sideways. That spooked Nikkolis and he jumped, before Lynn was quite in the saddle. When Nikkolis jumped, Lynn bumped his rump with his leg as he tried to swing on, and the gelding went to crow-hopping. Lynn was in a bad position, realizing that if he went off the horse, the saddle might continue slipping and go under Nikkolis' belly and spook him worse and he'd probably run and buck all the way home and maybe run through a fence and ruin himself, so he opted to try to ride it out. He never did get his other foot in the stirrup, but managed to bounce along and pull up the horse's head and stop him.

Lynn was pretty sore and bruised after bouncing along on that saddle for several jumps. It was an old Hamley saddle his dad bought in 1922 – one of those form-fitters with a high cantle and high pommel that held the rider right there, like sitting in a box. Lynn's dad rode that saddle for many years while he was out on the Wyoming desert herding sheep and catching feral horses. When he later gave the saddle to Lynn it had deep spur tracks across the cantle. When asked if he'd spurred the saddle getting on, he replied, "Hell no! Getting off!" So apparently the box effect was no guarantee against getting bucked off.

Some of the old cowboys thought those saddles were great for riding bucking horses, but Lynn was probably more bruised trying to stay on that horse than if he'd bailed off! Ordinarily Nikkolis wasn't a bucker, but he had great episodes of imaginative spooking, and was continually looking for boogies around the next corner, to make sure he saw them first, so they wouldn't get him.

Nikkolis leaping over the treacherous bridge.

He had keen eyesight, and a tremendous sense of smell and hearing. He noticed things in the far distance (a deer, another rider, a car moving along the highway in the valley five miles down the mountain from where we were checking cattle) long before I did. If my daughter Andrea and I split up to check cattle in a large range pasture, meeting again several hours later at a designated spot, he sensed her approach well before she and her horse came into sight over a hill. I could always tell which direction she'd be coming from; Nikkolis would become very intent on that horizon.

He also smelled or sensed any strange animals, pointing out a deer, badger or coyote before they came into view. One time he tensed up and centered all his attention on the trail ahead, and when we got around the corner of the mountain, a rattlesnake was sunning itself in the trail. No way could he have seen it; he must have smelled it.

I always preferred to ride him (rather than a more placid horse) when looking for cattle. He pointed out where they were, even if they were hiding in the brush or timber. If I paid attention to his body language and alertness, I could always find the cows.

Perhaps it was his extra-sensitivity that played havoc with his well-being and made him spooky – hearing and smelling things I couldn't. But like the boy who cried wolf, he also threw in some frustrating false alarms. Or maybe he just perceived some things as personal threats and I, being a dull human, just didn't understand.

I've tried to imagine the world as he saw it. What was it about a certain crossing on Baker Creek that inspired terror? The trail at that point goes around a little hill, and off to the side are some cottonwood trees. We saw a bear there once, but Nikkolis wasn't there on that occasion. But something about that grove of cottonwoods spooked him every time we went past it.

He made such a habit of these terror-stricken performances that my daughter and I jokingly made up "horrors" for those habitual spooks. We tried to match imagination with his. Perhaps there *were* bears in that cottonwood grove, but since we couldn't see them, maybe they were hiding behind the trees. They would have to be very thin bears, and quite agile--probably tall, thin bears that quickly sidled around the tree trunks as we rode by, keeping just out of our sight. Perhaps if we had stopped for a moment by the creek crossing we could even hear them growl!

But of course we couldn't stop that long because it was too scary. Nikkolis might try to balk and not cross that creek, but since that didn't work (I'd make him go across) he'd dance and prance through the crossing, ready to bolt, impatient to get far away from that terrifying place.

Nikkolis balking at a scary dry puddle.

Then there were the mud puddles. I never figured out what was so terrifying about mud puddles. If there was any possible way to walk around them rather than go through them (even to the point of being a contortionist) Nikkolis would manage to get around them and not muddy his feet. It was more than just a fetish about keeping his feet clean. There had to be an unseen ghastly horror lurking in that mud puddle – perhaps a slimy green alligator waiting with slavering jaws, ready to snap off any unsuspecting foot that inadvertently lands in that mud puddle. Nikkolis wasn't taking any chances. No way was he going to let any hoof of his stray into that puddle!

I could almost understand that little phobia. After all, there's no way to tell how deep a mud puddle really is, and there might be a grody, gruesome reptile lurking down there somewhere in the

185

depths. I can sympathize. As a child, I thought there might be monsters under the bed. If Nikkolis wanted to always make a scene at the mud puddles, I wasn't going to be sadistic and always force him to walk through them. That was nearly impossible; unless the puddle was huge, he always managed to maneuver around it anyway, being so agile – even if I tried to aim him right through it.

The only exception was when we chased cattle. At those times of urgency he was all business and knew his job. He knew that I knew that he knew he must get the cow, come hell or deep mud puddles. In those instances he'd keep charging at full speed, mud puddle or not, though it might take a slight nudge with my spur. He'd most likely jump it, unless it was too large, then he'd splash on through.

In the heat of battle he was a very loyal charger and always got his cow. His rider had to be a very good horseman on those cow-chasing experiences – riding him could be quite an uplifting experience. Like the time we tried to head off one old cow to keep her from going across a partly washed-out bridge. She was running the wrong direction and made a dash for the bridge to get away. She had a head start and barely beat us to the bridge and went on across. Nikkolis and I were going full tilt and there was no time to halt. It was one of those instances when you just keep going and mutter a quick prayer, and hope your horse doesn't put a foot down one of the holes in the bridge. He didn't. He didn't take that kind of chance.

He'd gone across that bridge a hundred times in the past, but didn't know it had partly washed out earlier that spring. Somehow he must have sensed the danger, and rather than take a chance, he merely leaped the whole thing – a broad jump of at least 15 feet. I wasn't expecting that kind of jump, and my riding form was less than perfect as we landed on the other side. But we made it over the bridge, caught up with the cow, and brought her back.

I can sort of understand his fear of big wet puddles that might contain lurking alligators in the murky bottom. But what I could never figure out was his fear of dry puddles. In his view, dry mud puddles were just as scary as wet ones.

I've tried to see it through Nikkolis' eyes. Perhaps if wet mud puddles harbor big wet alligators, maybe dry mud puddles have dry crocodiles lying in wait somewhere down under all those cracks and wrinkles of dried mud. I'm not sure what makes dry crocks more terrifying than wet ones. Maybe being dry they are smaller and livelier and more likely to bounce up and snap at an unsuspecting hoof. Or maybe, being dry, their teeth are sharper. I don't know. I gave up trying to figure it out. If anyone comes up with an answer as to why dry crocodiles and alligators are more deadly than wet ones, please let me know. Nikkolis never bothered to tell me.

KHAMIR
Farewell to My Little Girl's Horse

Khamir came into our lives April 28, 1973 – a sassy chestnut filly with four white feet and a white star-strip down her forehead – destined to be a horse for our young daughter Andrea. When our children were small, we wanted them each to have a horse of their own, so we bred two of our ranch mares for that purpose. One was my dear old Khamette, the first horse I raised myself, as a 4-H project. Khamir was her only foal, born when Khamette was 14.

Khamir was sassy and independent. Her disposition and attitude was more like that of her sire than her dam. Training her was a challenge. I wondered if she would ever become a dependable horse for our little girl. But Andrea (who by then was riding old Khamette, tagging along with me to ride range) loved the feisty filly. I spent a lot of time working with Khamir and gentling her, hoping that someday she'd be calm, well-mannered and trustworthy.

Andrea began riding Khamir a little when the young mare

was five and Andrea was eight. I was hesitant to have the two of them go off into the hills on their own; the sassy red mare was still a handful for a little girl. But the next year, when Andrea was more confident and the mare a little more dependable, Andrea did some range riding by herself. They were becoming a team.

At first, we'd start the ride together and I'd open and shut the gates (because the tight wire gates were difficult for a child) until we reached the range pastures where we needed to check cattle. Then we'd split up, to cover more territory, and meet again at a designated spot several hours later to eat lunch and compare notes. We each had our own hip-pocket "cow book"--a notebook with a list of all the cows. We'd mark off each cow and calf we saw that day, and try to see them all on every ride. We checked our cattle often on summer range, to make sure they were healthy (no foot rot, pinkeye, snakebite, or calves with pneumonia). If we discovered a sick animal we brought it home for medical attention. We also checked water troughs, fences, and gates. If gates got left open, cattle strayed into the wrong pastures and we'd have to look for them. If a cow or calf hadn't been seen for several days, we'd search until we found it.

At first I'd pray when Andrea took off over the mountain by herself on that mare, hoping she would not have any trouble or get bucked off. But she always managed just fine, and it gave her confidence, being able to do an important job by herself. She was becoming an excellent rider, and a lot of help with the cattle. She knew the cattle as well as I did, and could recognize a cow or calf from a distance without having to ride closer to read its tag number. She also had an intuitive feel for sickness and health in an animal, and I could trust her judgment. If she thought a case of pinkeye was serious enough to need treatment, or a calf looked a little dull and might be getting pneumonia, she was usually right.

She and Khamir became good at herding and chasing cattle. If we had to bring a pair home for some reason and the cow didn't want to leave the herd (making a mad dash for the brush or trying to get away from us), Andrea and her mare could handle their part of the job very well. We could always round up even the wildest cow.

By the time Andrea was nine, she sometime rode out by herself to check cattle on days I was too busy. She was strong enough by then to open and shut the difficult wire gates. And she could always manage to get back on Khamir, pulling herself up by the saddle strings to get her foot into that short little stirrup. She was proud of her mare the day she brought home a cow and calf all by herself; the cow needed treatment for pinkeye. It had been difficult herding the pair up out of brushy Baker Creek, over the mountain and through a gate, but she and her good little cowhorse had managed the job without any help.

They made a good team. But they had bad moments, too, like the time they were trying to head off a wild cow running full speed down a steep, rocky hillside. The cow was running down the mountain, trying to get into the timber to get away. Khamir tripped and fell, tumbling Andrea over her head. Luckily the child didn't land on a rock. She and the mare scrambled back to their feet, Andrea climbed back on, and they took off again full tilt after the cow. They caught up with the wayward bovine before she could disappear in the thick timber.

Another time when Khamir was still young and flighty, Andrea helped me gather cattle and move them to the next range pasture. We'd ridden for eight hours and had the cattle rounded up, moving

Andrea, age five, with her two-year-old filly, Khamir.

them along a creek bottom, taking them up toward the high range. The canyon was brushy and cows were going up both sides of the little creek.

Andrea decided to go across the creek to follow the cattle on the far side. There wasn't a good crossing; low-hanging branches made it impossible to ride across. So she got off the mare to lead her through the brush. Khamir was still inexperienced, and didn't want to step into the water. She jumped the little creek instead, landing on Andrea's leg.

I heard the child scream, so I jumped off my horse (Surrocco), tied him to one of the few available trees, and ran through the bushes to see what happened. I said a quick prayer and hoped Surrocco wouldn't set back (as he sometimes did) and take that old dead tree with him! Andrea was lying on the ground weeping. After assessing the damage and realizing her leg was not broken, we debated what to do. I asked her if she wanted to go home and put ice on the leg (it was starting to swell) but she said no, she wanted to finish moving the cows. So I caught her mare, helped her back on, and we rode for two more hard hours driving the cattle, Andrea riding with only one foot in a stirrup.

As the years went by, Andrea and Khamir went many miles together. Andrea enjoyed riding in the mountains, checking cattle and seeing wildlife. She and Khamir watched bobcats, coyotes, bighorn sheep (rare in our area), and bears, besides the usual deer, antelope, and elk – and one mountain lion.

Andrea especially enjoyed seeing the elk. Often she'd get very close to them, like the time she and Khamir rode into a large group of elk cows with calves. The calves were confused, never having seen a horse before, and some ran up to her horse--making their high pitched "eeep eeep" noises. Another time she and Khamir were on a hillside watching a group of elk run down the mountain, when Khamir suddenly snorted and spun around. A big bull elk had come up right behind them.

One year Khamir suffered a stone bruise trotting through sharp rocks. She was lame and needed several weeks' time off from work. So we bred her that summer, and the next year she had a colt, named Khamahn (nicknamed Veggie – more about him in another chapter). A couple years later Andrea was training a young mare and had another horse to ride--and decided to raise a few more foals from Khamir. She had two more colts, Diablo and Fozzy.

Diablo was sired by a little bay Arabian stallion that we borrowed from friends. We kept him on the ranch for a few weeks to breed a couple mares. Diablo was black, like his great-grandmother Scrappy, and a very sweet colt. Andrea trained him herself and he was a joy to ride. Lynn and I both rode him a few times. His pleasant disposition and eagerness to please reminded me a lot of his grandmother Khamette and he was a horse anybody could ride.

He liked Lynn and every time Andrea and I met him on the road in the pickup or on his motorbike when Lynn was irrigating, Diablo wanted to stop and get a pet from Lynn, even if it meant sticking his nose in the pickup window. One day we were moving cattle out of the Withington Creek canyon and Lynn had driven up on his motorcycle to check on us, and went along with us the rest of the way, even though he was wearing his irrigating boots. The motorcycle made it along the rocky trails okay but Andrea had to help Lynn get it up the steep hill over the top, and I led Diablo from my horse.

He was always fun to ride, and had a humorous habit of bird-watching. He's the only horse I've known that always looked up at birds and airplanes overhead. Sometimes he'd be watching them so intently he didn't notice where he was putting his feet! He was a unique and special character. Then we lost him tragically when he was only eight years old.

Andrea and I had been riding range, moving cattle to the middle range pasture and moving some of their salt. On the way home, Diablo started to colic. It was mild colic, not violent, but he didn't improve.

We gave him Banamine when we got home. He colicked off and on through the next day, and the vet recommended that we bring him in to the clinic. He'd never ridden in a trailer before, but a friend loaned us his three-horse trailer, and we hauled him to town. He trusted Andrea completely, and even in his pain and misery he went willingly into the trailer with her. She rode with him in the trailer, comforting him.

He spent the night at the clinic, on medication and IVs, and Andrea stayed with him, but there wasn't much else the vet could do for him because he wasn't set up to do colic surgery. With Diablo's symptoms the vet suspected a piece of small intestine might be caught between the liver and another organ. There really wasn't anything else he could do for Diablo and we couldn't afford the gamble of hauling him to an equine hospital 170 miles away – a trip he might not survive--and several thousand dollars for surgery. So brought him back home and hoped for the best – and kept him as comfortable as possible. But within a few hours we realized it was hopeless, and mercifully put him down after Andrea spent some time with him in a tearful good-by.

After having Diablo and Fozzy (his story in a later chapter), Andrea was still hoping for a filly from Khamir, to continue on with that family of horses, so we bred her again. But that dream was not to be.

The old mare was due to foal in about a month, and we didn't quite have the foaling pen ready. A yearling filly was living in it temporarily and I was figuring out another place for her so that we could clean out the pen for Khamir to foal. I always put our pregnant mares in pens next to the house, under the yard light, so I can watch them at night as their time comes to foal. We planned to move Khamir from her little pasture and put her by the house where I could watch her more closely.

I went out that Sunday morning early to feed the horses, and found Khamir lying in her pasture, dead. She had lain down to sleep or to roll, and ended up with her back slightly downhill on

Andrea and Khamir moving cattle in the winter.

a small slope. Being heavily pregnant and clumsy, she probably was unable to get up; pressure from her big belly caused her to suffocate, so we lost both her and the baby.

If only she hadn't lain on the slope. If only we'd had her in the foaling pen (a more level spot--and I could have peeked at her a few times during the night, from my window). If only it had happened during the day, when we could have seen her and helped her get up. My mind was churning over all the "what ifs", all the things we could have done differently.

But life isn't like a tape you can rewind past a certain place and start over. So with tears streaming down my face I trudged back to the house to wake the rest of the family and break the sad news, and let Andrea have some time alone with her old friend to say goodbye. The two of them grew up together, and the parting wasn't easy. As Lynn and I buried Khamir in the old garden spot later that day, hundreds of memories flooded back, of our little girl growing up and learning to ride, becoming my best cow-chasing partner and range-riding buddy, on her sassy chestnut mare.

It was the end of an era. With Khamir gone, it was also the end of that family of ranch horses. Khamir was Khamette's only foal, and Khamir's foals were all boys. Geldings. They were the last of the line. It was also the end of another era. Our little girl had grown up and was ready to launch out on a life of her own. Khamir was a part of her childhood and youth, now gone. A chapter of life finished. The mare's passing came as a sort of punctuation mark, emphasizing the fact that my little girl's childhood was past. But what they shared together – what we all shared – will be with us forever. Wistful thoughts. Good memories. Special times.

I'm grateful that Khamir and Andrea made such a good team, grateful that even though the mare was at times a difficult challenge for the child, Andrea had the spunk and determination necessary to be able to meet that challenge, and gain confidence and ability. A youngster needs to reach for some goals, attempt some tasks that may seem too big – especially in the eyes of parents who worry that the child can't handle it. We don't want to see the child get hurt. But if we overprotect our children and wait until WE think they are ready for a hard task, they may lose interest. We need to let them reach for the stars, try those challenges, and have some successes that give them confidence, self-assurance and satisfaction – and make us proud of them. Our children need that quest, to accomplish something that makes us proud.

Andrea was a timid little girl who took on the challenge of a naughty, feisty chestnut filly. Together they worked through all

Andrea and Khamir check cattle in the fall on our 320-acre mountain pasture.

the problems and became a team, helping each other grow into their fullest potential. That mare was special. I know that Andrea's memories of growing up in our family here on the ranch will always be intertwined with memories of Khamir. And Khamir will always have a very special place in my heart, as well.

SADIE AND SNICKERS
Challenging Sisters

I really liked the Arab-Thoroughbred crosses as ranch horse/cow horses because of their endurance, intelligence and agility – partly because all the foals from our old Thoroughbred mare Nell were so exceptional in these attributes. They spoiled me, and I wanted to raise more good horses of similar bloodlines. Nell was gone (died peacefully of old age) and her daughters could not carry on the line; Fahleen died young before I had a chance to raise a foal from her, and Nikki had only one foal – Nikkolis, a gelding. We tried twice to raise another foal from Nikki, but she didn't settle.

So I was looking for another good Thoroughbred mare, to breed to my sister's Arabian stallion. There are very few Thoroughbreds in our area (Quarter Horse country), so I asked my sister (who lived in Oregon) to see if she could find one. She located a 6-year-old Thoroughbred mare named Goodnight Katy (sired by a stallion named Key to the Gun and out of a mare named Bedtime Story). This mare had gone through several owners and was sold to my sister by someone who'd bred her to an Arabian stallion to raise an endurance horse. The mare was for sale again, for reasons I later discovered. But at that point I agreed to buy her, sight unseen. My sister foaled her out (the filly was born in March 1983), and rebred her to Surrabu, then hauled the pregnant mare (with foal at side) to our ranch.

I had plans for those two foals (the filly at side, and the unborn baby); one would be a horse for me, and the other for my daughter to train and ride. Her mare Khamir was 10 years old by then, and Andrea wanted to raise a foal, to have a younger horse coming on as a future cowhorse.

Goodnight Katy arrived June 19 with her foal, a dark bay filly I named Sadie. The filly was three months old by the time my sister was able to haul the pair over here from Oregon. She was wild and hard to catch. My sis hadn't had time to do much with her – except treat her for a navel infection during her first two weeks of life. So her only experience with humans was the trauma of being caught, wrestled and doctored. She was wary, untrusting and not about to let anyone sneak up on her.

I didn't like the idea of leaving a halter on a foal; it's dangerous if the foal catches it on anything or puts a hind foot through it scratching an ear. But I left one on Sadie for a few days so I could get hold of her. At first it took two of us to corner her in the pen with her mama. I began leading lessons immediately, then tying lessons.

Sadie had a very independent, anti-social attitude. The Thoroughbred mare was fairly mellow, but also a bit wary and independent. She didn't like her feet handled. When I tried to trim her feet she didn't want anyone picking up her hind feet. Her former owners used a lip chain when trimming or shoeing her. A lip chain is similar to a nose twitch in the resulting effect;

by putting pressure on certain areas it stimulates release of endorphins, which tend to calm and sedate the horse.

I tried to trim the mare's hind feet, but she'd jerk and try to pull them away, shaking me around like a rag doll. She was worse about the right hind, determined to not have it handled. I could trim the left one, if I did it quickly. Since I wasn't going to ride her and didn't need to shoe her, we eventually came to a truce/compromise. She would cock that right hind foot (resting it on the toe) and allow me to reach down and trim it all the way around with hoof nippers, except the toe that was resting on the ground. The toe could wear off a bit on its own. She didn't mind that method of trimming – as long as I didn't try to pick up her foot!

S adie was a difficult pupil. Her early training wasn't easy, but she did learn to lead, tie, and have her feet handled. She was as reluctant as her mother to have her feet picked up, but at that point I was stronger than she was, and she couldn't take them away from me. I kept trying to win her confidence and trust, but she was never very friendly.

My first priority was to get her over her fear. She learned that if she was calm and didn't fight, I would then put the foot back down. By the time she was a yearling I could pick up all four feet and trim them, though at first it was just one swipe at a time with the rasp, and then put the foot back down.

I planned to start riding her a little as a two-year-old, but an injury foiled those plans. By that time she was living in a small pasture with her younger sister. When I went out one morning in mid-April to feed them, Sadie was lame and weak. She'd sliced all the skin off the front and side of her right hind cannon from hock to hoof – with a deep hole down past the bone below the hock-- and had bled a lot. The cut barely missed the main tendon. She must have done it early in the night because the blood was dry and the flap of skin was dead and dry. The leg was already swollen.

Lynn helped me doctor the wound and snip some dead skin off. We walked around the fence to see where she'd gotten caught but there were no bad places or stretched or broken wires. She might have rolled too close to one of the braces – and got a hind leg stuck up between the brace wires and sliced the leg in her struggle to get free. No other part of the fence could have withstood her struggles without some evidence.

We treated the wound twice a day for a couple days then realized we had to get the rest of the dead skin cut away, but Sadie was too skittish to allow it. I called a vet. Liz was an intern at a local clinic, planning to specialize in horses. She had to tranquilize Sadie to work on the leg, but Sadie was still uncooperative and Liz had to put her clear "out" on the ground. Then she clipped off the rest of the dead skin and cleaned up the wound – which was down to the bone – filled the gash with antibiotic ointment, wrapped it with gauze, and bandaged the leg. She gave Sadie penicillin, bute and a tetanus shot. I trimmed her hind feet while she was still "out" because I knew it would be a long time before I could handle them again for trimming.

We kept her on antibiotics (daily injections) to make sure she didn't get a bone infection, and bute for a week to reduce swelling and inflammation. Everything was fine until we had to change the bandage a few days later. Sadie would *not* let us handle the leg. It took two hours to get that bandage off and another one on. The next time was just as traumatic. Finally we just left it uncovered and applied antibiotic ointment and squirted an antiseptic solution into the deep hole under her hock.

When it finally started to heal and fill in, I put alum powder on the wound daily to keep it from developing proud flesh. Alum is the white powder used in making pickles, and an astringent that works nicely to retard proud flesh. This was a lot easier (and less caustic) than the old medications for proud flesh that I'd used on Nell's wire cuts in the early 1960s. Sadie didn't mind me spreading a little alum over the raw area without having to handle her leg. Since it didn't hurt, she didn't try to move away or kick.

I handled her often, trying to build a bond of trust, but she still was a very untrusting horse. That fall I saddled her a few times with a small child's saddle, but she didn't like it. The leg was healed by spring, when she was three, so I refreshed all our lessons in groundwork – leading, longeing, saddling, bridling, giving to pressure from a bit, turning in each direction.

She still didn't like the saddle, and when I tried to lead her around with it, she bucked. So before I started riding her, I began ponying her with the saddle on, leading her from Brownie. I ponied her for several weeks, leading her all over the low range, through the creek and gullies, around and through the sagebrush and up and down the hills.

When she finally seemed at ease with the saddle, I started riding her in the small pen by our house – after first ponying her to try to get her tired. She didn't want to stand still for me to get on, even after I put weight in the stirrup a few times with Lynn holding her for me. So Lynn held her for me to mount, and put his hand over her eye to block her vision so she wouldn't freak out at the movement of me getting on. Andrea was on Brownie,

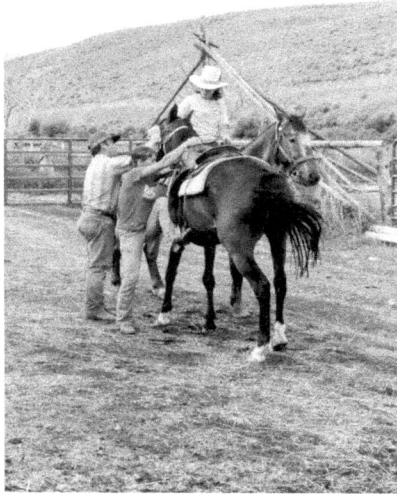

Mounting Sadie for the first time.

snuggled up close to Sadie on the other side so she was boxed in and couldn't move much as I carefully mounted.

The next day I mounted her the same way (after ponying first), then encouraged her to take a few steps. She snorted and tensed up. We made a few circles around the pen and she jumped around but didn't buck. I got her calm and went a few more steps and ended on that good note. The next day we made a few more trips around the pen.

The fourth day's lesson went well, and the next day I rode her briefly up the lane and back. The next day, however, when I started to get on she took off bucking as soon as I was in the saddle. She bucked around the pen several times as I tried to keep her head up, and was about to crash into the metal gate when I finally went off – and pulled her over when I went off. She fell down hard on her side, then got up and went running around the pen. I caught her and got on and off again. I realized I should have had her head tied up to the saddle horn; maybe she wouldn't have been able to buck so hard.

Later that day I rode her again, this time with halter rope tied to the horn, and side reins snapped to the halter so I could readily pull her head to the side with those as well as the bit. I pulled her in a tight circle each time she tried to buck. When she settled down and walked calmly we ended the lesson, on a good note.

I rode her every day the rest of the summer, but she never became dependable. Andrea hiked along with me the first rides out, and then rode with me and we took her up on the range, checking cattle. She still didn't like to be mounted. The only way I could mount her without someone holding her was to pull her head toward me as I got on, spinning her around so she couldn't buck. I tried to wear her out on our rides, hoping she might stand still as I mounted and dismounted multiple times after we got home, but she never did stand still. She was a little better after a long ride on a hot day, but not great.

The next spring, when she was four, I planned to pony her before getting on her, but the first time I put my saddle on she tried to buck it off. She was the most frustrating young horse I'd tried to train. The sad thing about giving up on her was that she had a lot of talent – agile, surefooted – and tremendous endurance. She proved that trait when I was trying to wear her out the summer she was 3, and couldn't. She was one tough filly.

Reluctantly, I sold her – to a rodeo contractor buying potential bucking horses for high school rodeo. She bucked, but not enough to suit him, and he sold her to an outfit in Nevada that needed horses that could cover big country. I heard later that Sadie was able to go the distance, but the gal who rode her (an excellent horsewoman) never felt comfortable with her. Sadie was *not* a user-friendly horse!

Goodnight Katy's second foal was due in April 1984. It was cold, and we put a windbreak in one of the calving pens – where we could check on her during the night, from the house. We had a blizzard two days before she foaled. She started labor just after midnight April 21 and was taking too long; one leg was back, probably hung up at the elbow on the mare's pelvis. We pulled on that leg, and then the foal was born – a nice bay filly. She had a small white marking on her forehead but no other white except for an unusual gray mottling on one front fetlock.

The weather was cold so we dried her with towels. When she tried to nurse, she was so tall and long-legged she had trouble finding the udder. We tried for two hours to help her find a teat, and finally milked colostrum from the mare and fed the foal a bottle, then tried to guide her to a teat with the bottle nipple. She still stubbornly refused, so we milked more from Katy, and fed her with the bottle and went back to bed. Two hours later she was still trying unsuccessfully, so we went back out and finally got her on a teat.

After that, things went well, and Andrea tried to handle the foal a little every day. Since Katy's older filly was such a handful, with a less-than-amenable attitude, we'd decided this new foal would be Andrea's horse. We hoped this new baby, with Surrabu as the sire, would be more user-friendly and trainable than Sadie.

Andrea named the foal Snickers. She was friendlier than Sadie, but independent and sassy. She was a good learning experience for Andrea, as the first horse she trained from the very beginning.

When Snickers was a month old she cut her face (probably on the fence), slicing it just above her left eye. The lump/flap of skin hanging there wasn't something that could be stitched, so we cut it off. Andrea and Lynn held the filly, with a hand over her eye, and I quickly snipped the flap off with my sharpest hoof nippers – washed and disinfected – in one quick motion before she could jump away. That worked, and the area healed with a small scar.

Andrea gave the foal leading lessons with butt rope. Tying lessons were more of a challenge. She liked to pull back. We used a body rope (around her girth) so some of the strain and stress would be on her whole body and not all on her head and neck.

When Snickers was a yearling Andrea spent more time working with her, and handling her feet. The filly was stubborn and would try to take her foot away, or lean on her, or sink down toward the ground just to test her and see if she could make Andrea let go, but Andrea was tenacious and held on.

That summer she did a lot of leading, tying and taught her to longe. Andrea led her up and down the lane, and up the horse trail above our house. One day a deer jumped out of the brush, and Snickers spooked and tried to bolt away. She bumped into Andrea and pushed her off the trail into the rocks below, but Andrea hung onto the rope and pulled Snickers down to her. She was determined to hang onto that filly.

On another leading lesson, Andrea and I took our fillies across a shallow ditch. The first time over it, Snickers jumped, to keep up with me and Sadie since we had gone on ahead. On the way back,

First ride on Sadie.

however, Snickers refused to cross. She was smart and knew there was a culvert farther up the ditch; she wanted to walk across it instead of across the ditch. My attempts at encouraging her from behind with swats on the rump with my lead rope were spooking my filly, so I led Sadie home and tied her up, then came back to help Andrea – who didn't want to let Snickers get away with this kind of refusal. The headstrong filly would just keep challenging her young owner unless Andrea could instill more respect.

With encouragement from behind, Snickers realized she *could* cross the ditch. After she started walking calmly across it instead of angrily jumping it, we ended the lesson. She just needed to realize that Andrea was the team leader.

Andrea diligently led her out on the trails and in the fields, leading her at the walk and trot, positioned at the filly's shoulder (with about 10 inches of rope between hand and halter) so she had

207

good leverage. When the filly tried to go too fast or bolt, Andrea was able to use body leverage to pull her head around by bracing her arm and elbow against Snicker's shoulder.

At that time I was writing for *Horseman* magazine and they asked me do a series on Andrea training Snickers. We took photos of Andrea working with the filly, leading her, cleaning her feet, ponying lessons, starting her first rides. The spring she was two, Snickers was a handful after six months winter vacation. The fillies were living together, and the first time Andrea led her away from Sadie, she threw a fit. Similarly, when we tied Snickers and led Sadie away, Snickers threw another fit. Our goal was to wean them away from each other so they'd realize they didn't have to always be together.

Snickers had to learn to mind her manners and pay attention to her person, and not use Sadie as an excuse to set back on the rope or walk all over the person handling her. We also started ponying Snickers a little from Brownie. While I was writing the series for *Horseman*, Andrea got some fan mail. One letter was from Misty Couture, a girl her age who also had a young horse. Misty lived in Dawson River in Yukon Territory, Canada. They started a correspondence that lasted many years and they still keep in touch.

For Snickers' first rides I rode her in the pen a few times, and then a few times out in the hills. On one of those rides a jackrabbit took off from a sagebrush right in front of her and Snickers whirled and bolted straight up the hill before I got her stopped. Then as we continued home we were on a very narrow trail along a steep hillside and she wasn't paying attention to her footing. She fell off the trail and floundered down the steep hill. I feared she would fall and roll clear to the bottom, but she kept her feet under her and we realized she was actually quite agile!

Andrea started riding her with snaffle reins and reins snapped to the halter – to have good control without so much pressure on her mouth – and halter rope tied up to the saddle horn in case she decided to buck. I went along on Brownie at first, then Surrocco, because Snickers got along better with him. Those two were a lot alike, being half-siblings (by Surrabu). He was a calm influence when she spooked, or had to pass a car for the first time along the road as we were going or coming from the range pastures.

One time we couldn't help her very much however, coming down the road from our upper place. One neighbor has a small acreage along the road, with a pond. He pumped out of the pond and had a sprinkler going, spraying across the road, making a swishing noise. That upset Snickers a little, but when a bunch of geese came honking out onto the road and flapping their wings, Snickers lost it, and spun around. Andrea was hanging out over midair with all her weight in one stirrup and holding onto that rein, and probably would have been able to regain her balance except that the rein broke! When that happened, she was flung onto the ground, flat on her back. She lay there a moment, the breath knocked out of her, and I feared she may have injured her back. I checked on her and she sat up and said she was ok, so I took off after her horse.

Snickers had galloped away from the scary, obnoxious geese, straight up the hill above the road. I galloped after her, and she stopped and let me catch her and lead her back to Andrea. We improvised a "fix" on her broken rein and she was able to ride home, in spite of a bad headache – probably a mild concussion from hitting the back of her head on the hard ground and rocks.

Andrea and Snickers went quite a few miles during the late summer of 1986, and we sometimes rode the two fillies together (two-year-old Snickers and three-year-old Sadie).

The next year, when Snickers was three, she started riding range in earnest, and Snickers soon proved to be a good cowhorse. Andrea started riding the filly by herself that year and she and Snickers made a good team. One day they came across an ornery Angus bull that was trying to come back into our range. She and I together had chased him back to his proper range the first time. When Andrea saw him again, he wasn't quite through the fence yet. There wasn't a gate she could go through to chase him away, so she got off and crawled through the fence to throw rocks at him to chase him down off the hill into the timber. The bull turned on her and threatened her a few times but she yelled and threw rocks at him and he went on down the mountain. Snickers ran up and down the fence, wanting to come help Andrea. When she finally got home that day I was waiting on the porch, worrying. I'd had a really bad feeling that she was in danger.

A few days later Andrea was checking cattle and found the bull back in our range again. This time after she got him back through a gate she took him farther – about six miles. He turned on her three or four times, but Snickers would pin her ears back and gallop right into him and bite him and he'd keep going. The last time, when he turned on her, Andrea and Snickers were on a steep hill above him.

Andrea jumped off and grabbed a big rock, climbed back in the saddle and threw it at him while mounted – and luckily hit him! He turned around and kept going down the mountain. She

Leading lessons – Snickers was a handful for Andrea as a yearling.

and Snickers bonded as a team, early on, during their many solo range rides and cattle chases.

We had one of my sister's Arabian stallions here for a couple of years – a son of Surrabu and therefore a half-brother to Snickers – and bred some mares to him. While he was here, Andrea rode him occasionally as a spare horse, to give Snickers a day off. He was tough and could go all day. One day, however, he got colicky on the way home. Fortunately she was only two miles from home and got off and led him. Lynn was coming down the road on his motorbike, from irrigating, and saw she had a problem. He came to get me (and a shot of Banamine) for the stallion. Andrea continued leading him, and he worked out of the gut cramps by the time she got home.

A few weeks later she rode him on a long cow-checking ride and he colicked again, more violently this time. She was up Baker Creek on the high range. He threw himself down so quickly the first time, she didn't have time to dismount. She tucked and rolled to get away from him, but he rolled over and hit her in the back with his hind feet (freshly shod; I'd just put new shoes on him the day before!).

She led him a little, but he was throwing himself to the ground so hard, trying to roll, that she was afraid he would ruin her saddle. She took it off and left it in a meadow in Baker Creek and led him the rest of the way home, about four miles down out of the mountains.

She had to retrieve her saddle, so she opted to ride Snickers up there bareback to get it. Snickers was still young and goofy, and Andrea had never ridden her bareback but was confident that it would be ok. I rode with her, to open gates for her, and to make sure she didn't get dumped off! She did fine, however, retrieved her saddle, and we rode home. She and Snickers were well bonded by that time, and trusted each other.

After that episode, we figured out the reason for her brother's colic. There was a big crab-apple tree at the top corner of his pen, and the apples were falling into his pen. He loved to eat them and they didn't seem to bother him except when he was being ridden! Exercise and crab apples seemed to create a belly ache (which we found on a couple other occasions with other horses). So we fenced off that corner where the crab-apples were, and he had no more colic problems.

Snickers showed her heart and athletic ability when we were bringing a cow home through the brushy creek bottom. The cow ran into the brush just below a big tree that had blown down. Andrea and Snickers knew they would lose her if they took the extra time to go clear around the down tree, so Snickers jumped it. With its

Andrea riding range on Snickers.

huge trunk and branches it was impossible to clear the whole thing, but Snickers didn't hesitate; she landed on the big trunk and made another jump to the other side, and headed the cow.

She also proved her worth the year we were moving cows to the middle range after several days of rain. The ground was muddy and slick, and it was still raining. Lynn and I were unable to help that day; we both had severe diarrhea. Andrea went alone to help Kosslers (our range neighbors) move all our cattle and theirs. To keep dry, she was wearing a floppy felt hat and a big slicker. Snickers was still pretty skittish and not used to flapping slickers. We worried that Andrea might have trouble getting on after opening the gate to go out there and meet up with Kosslers but she did fine.

She had to do most of the sorting because it was too slick and treacherous for most of the other horses. Snickers just kept galloping through the mud, doing sliding stops heading a cow or calf. She had to outrun one that took off the wrong way, running to the brush along the little creek. Snickers just broad-jumped the brush hedge and got the cow. Andrea lost her hat in the wind and rain had to go back the next day and find it.

Snickers was Andrea's best cowhorse, and also her best learning experience. Snickers was for Andrea like Nell was for me when I was her age – having to learn the patience, finesse and trust to handle a super-intelligent high-strung athletic horse.

Snickers and Andrea had a bond that enabled them to do great things together. They went many places that she's never taken any other horse, and did many adventurous things, in rugged terrain. Snickers enjoyed exploring new places as much as Andrea did and packed home a lot of elk horns that they stumbled across in their many travels.

Then as she got older, her knees and back were painful and she wasn't as agile anymore. Eventually Snickers was retired and Andrea was riding Breezy. By the summer of 2013 when she was 29, Snickers was losing some of her sight and hearing. So that fall we put her down – along with Fozzy (Andrea's other special horse) – and buried them together.

KATY DOLL
The Quirky Mare with a Big Heart

One hot day in June 1985, when Andrea was 15 and her good mare Khamir was 12, we'd been checking cows and gates – a long day of range riding. Trotting home, Khamir hit a sharp rock with her left front foot and began limping so we walked the rest of the way. She'd stone bruised it pretty badly and needed some time off for it to heal.

During summer we generally rode every day, and it was best to have a couple horses to trade off so they wouldn't have to go every day. Andrea had Brownie to ride, but needed a replacement for Khamir until she got over the stone bruise. We looked around for another horse and heard that Royden Capps, a rancher up Hayden Creek, had a seven-year-old mare to sell, that was closely related to some of our horses.

The mare was named Katy Doll. She was sired by Royden's stallion, a son of Sur Amir (Khamir's sire) that was out of an El Khamis daughter. Thus Katy's grandmother on her sire's side (the El Khamis daughter) was a half-sister to Khamette, Nikki, Fahleen, and Ahmahl. Katy's mother was a Quarter Horse/Saddlebred cross.

When we drove up Hayden Creek to look at the mare, Royden had her saddled and bridled and tied to the fence. She was a nice looking chestnut mare with a white blaze and white socks. I rode her around the barnyard, and then Andrea rode her around, and liked her, so we bought her. She was a little too wide in the front end and had a hard time going down steep hills very fast, but on relatively level ground she was quick as a cat and great for sorting cattle.

After we got her home, we realized why Royden had her already caught, saddled and bridled. She was ear-shy and did *not* want anyone touching her ears, which made her difficult to bridle. Andrea spent that first summer getting Katy over that phobia, by taking the bridle apart at the side buckle and putting the crown piece up over her neck behind her ears without having to touch them. Within a few months of patient non-confrontational bridling, the mare got over her phobia and we were able to bridle her in the conventional manner.

Andrea rode her the rest of the summer, alternating between Katy and Brownie as her main cowhorses that year. One problem, however, was that Katy hadn't been ridden for a few years and was hog fat when we got her. With all that fat, and tender girth skin because she hadn't been ridden, Katy developed a serious cinch sore. We started using neoprene girths (easier on the skin than the old string cinches), but Katy's sore was hard to clear up.

Andrea rode her bareback for most of two years – riding range, chasing cattle, sorting cattle. Katy had fairly sharp withers, however, which could be uncomfortable on a long, hard ride. One day when Lynn went up the creek road on his motorbike and met us coming home from the high range (seven miles from our house),

Andrea and Katy.

Andrea mentioned this problem, and Lynn came home and got a foam pillow for her. From then on, Andrea often used that little foam pad, in an old pillowcase (that we could wash periodically). It didn't take long for Andrea to get Katy ready to ride – just bridle her, put the pillow on her back and go.

Riding bareback, without stirrups, improved Andrea's riding skills and balance. Even today, she credits those years riding Katy bareback as giving her the ability to "stay with" a horse under all kinds of circumstances. The only time she ever fell off Katy was during a hard cow chase when the mare stumbled and fell down, dumping Andrea on the ground in front of her. This was during the tough cow chase when she and I were galloping back and forth across the mountainside, trying to halt the flow of cattle pouring down the ridge into the wrong place (episode mentioned in the Surrocco chapter).

HORSE TALES

Our horses were tired from a long day's cattle gather and then had to spend two more hours galloping back and forth to stop those cattle and head them around the hill instead of on down the ridges. Andrea and Katy were holding up their end of it pretty well but Katy was getting really tired so Surrocco and I were making longer, harder runs. I'd gone around the hill to head a few more cows and on my way back with those cattle I saw Katy standing there, head down, with Andrea in a crumpled heap at her feet. My heart stopped; I thought the child was seriously injured or worse.

I galloped over to them and Andrea slowly picked herself up and leaned against the panting mare. She told me Katy had been running downhill as hard as she could go, to head another cow, stumbled, and Andrea went off over her head. The mare's front feet slid into Andrea's ribs, but didn't hurt her. A tribute to that mare's athletic ability, to literally stop on a dime as she stumbled, not wanting to step on Andrea.

She got back on Katy and we continued our cow chasing, and fortunately were just about done (only a few more cows trickling down the mountain), because our horses were just about done. We got the job accomplished, however, and let our horses walk slowly all the way home (about four miles) to cool out. Katy didn't have as much endurance as Surrocco or our other Anglo-Arabs, but she certainly had as much heart. She was the best cowhorse Andrea ever had, for sorting cattle on the flat. She didn't have the endurance of Snickers but she had a quicker burst of speed cutting cows.

We bred Katy in 1986 to the same gray Arabian stallion we'd bred Khamir to the year before – and she had a chestnut filly in 1987 that later turned gray. We named that filly Sharah (pronounced shuh-rah`) but started calling her Rubber-lips. Rubbie for short.

Andrea and Katy sorting cattle in the field.

That name stuck, and she was always Rubbie after that. Rubbie was easy to train, and had a lot of endurance when I started riding range with her. She was my best cowhorse for many years, after Nikkolis was gone.

We bred Katy again in 1988, to a little bay Arabian stallion. The next spring she had a gangly bay colt we named Brumby. Khamir was bred to that same stallion, and had a nice black colt that Andrea named Diablo. Brumby and Diablo lived together as weanlings and grew up together.

In 1989 we had another stallion on the ranch for a while, a son of Surrabu, and bred Katy again. In 1990 Katy had a nice-looking bay filly from that breeding, named Miss Piggy. We tried one more time to breed her, but she didn't settle, so after her stint as a broodmare she went back to being part of the work string, as a spare horse for riding range and cattle work.

By that time Michael was married and he and his wife Carolyn lived here on the ranch for a while before they moved to the Boise area. That fall we had all our bulls in a big pasture on the lower place, and one day the fence got torn down between that field and our neighbor's place – probably from his bulls fighting with ours. Our bulls had gone down into his field. Andrea wasn't home that day, so Carolyn helped me round up the bulls, and she rode Katy.

As she saddled the mare (using Andrea's saddle) and tightened the cinch, the leather latigo strap broke. That was a stroke of luck – having it break *before* she was riding and galloping around after the bulls, or she could have had a serious wreck. We quickly found another latigo strap to replace the broken one, and then Carolyn and I rode down to sort out the mess with the bulls. Lynn went on his 4-wheeler to help guard the hole in the fence that was temporarily serving as a gate as we sorted our bulls out of the neighbor's herd (running round and round through the brush) and brought groups of them back to our field. Katy was always good at working cattle, and gave it her whole heart. She and Carolyn were good help and we eventually got all our bulls sorted out of the neighbor's cattle and herded back through the fence – and Lynn put the fence back together again.

One winter a few years later Katy was living in a pen by the creek and on a cold, stormy morning in December when I fed the horses I saw that she was ill. She hadn't eaten all of her hay from the night before, and was shivering and shaking, cold and wet from the snow and clammy sweat, and she had diarrhea. I brought her out of her pen into the back yard and found an old horse blanket to put on her, and called the vet. It looked to me like she needed IV fluids, but when the vet arrived, he thought that the oral fluids

Andrea moving cows on Katy.

and medication he gave her by stomach tube would be adequate.

She continued to go downhill, however, and we put her in the barn, out of the cold, and called the vet back again that evening. He started her on IV fluids at that time, and we stayed there in the barn all night changing the IV bags, putting on new ones as the old ones became empty, but by then it was too late. She died before morning. The vet was never sure what caused the sudden and acute diarrhea (it was a little late in the season to be Potomac Horse Fever), but it was fast and it was deadly.

We were devastated by the sudden loss of a good mare, but she left us with a good replacement. Even though we'd sold Brumby (as a three-year-old that I'd started in training) and Miss Piggy (as an untrained two-year-old) to a lady and her daughter in Montana, we still had Rubbie – Katy's first foal, born in 1987. Rubbie (three-quarters Arab, sired by the little gray stallion) was already becoming my best cowhorse, as a replacement for Nikkolis. Rubbie had Katy's quickness, speed and agility for sorting cattle, with a little more endurance – and served me well as my main cowhorse for nearly 20 years (until she was 23 years old). I still rode her occasionally until this last summer when she and her older brother (Khamir's son) became fully retired at age 27 and 28. So Katy, the emergency replacement horse for Andrea to ride, that summer long ago, left a lasting legacy and was much appreciated as part of our family of ranch horses.

VEGGIE
From Goofball to Kid Horse

When Khamir went lame with a stone bruise, we bought Katy for Andrea to ride, and bred Khamir. We liked the endurance and intelligence of Arabians, so we looked around for an Arabian stallion. There weren't very many in our area, since most people have Quarter Horses. We found a nice gray stallion, owned by Wendy Aldous, who lived near the ranch where Lynn grew up. The stallion was a well-mannered little fellow, and Wendy's father (Arthur Aldous) said we could bring our mare any time and put her in his corral. When Khamir came into heat we loaded her in our stock truck (since we didn't have a horse trailer), and took Nikki along to keep her company – since Khamir had never ridden in a truck or trailer. There was a loading dock at the Aldous ranch so we could unload the mares.

We got Khamir bred and she was due to foal the next year in May. She started developing an udder by mid-May and we put her in one of the pens next to the house, under the yardlight, where we could watch her. When we went to Michael's high school graduation, we asked one of our neighbors, Marcy Neal, if she would watch Khamir for us that evening. We didn't want anything to go wrong while we were gone, since Khamir was 13 and this was her first foal. We told Marcy that if there was any problem she should call our veterinarian.

Khamir didn't foal that night, but waited until the next morning. The foal wasn't coming very readily, however, and Lynn and I gave it a little pull. Once the shoulders passed through the birth canal, the birth was easily accomplished. The foal was a chestnut colt with a narrow blaze/strip down his face (he later turned gray). Khamir was unsure about motherhood at first, until the foal was up and nursing.

Andrea and I gave him an enema (he was having trouble passing meconium) and started the gentling process, getting him used to being handled by humans. When he was a couple days old we put a little halter on him and led him (using a rope around his rump to encourage him to come along) and mama into the back yard so Khamir could graze, and started handling his feet, picking them up.

Since his mom was Khamir, we named him Khamahn ("come 'ere" and "come on" as mama and baby). But he soon got a nickname. Michael started calling him "vegetable" for fun, and then we all started calling him "Veggie" and the name stuck.

He was a lively, hyper little fellow. Andrea led him a lot, but one of the first times she took him up our lane he spooked and took off, trying to run back down to his mother who was tied in the barnyard. Andrea didn't let go, even after she couldn't quite keep up with his sprinting take-off and ended up tripping and dragging along on her belly before she got him stopped! By the time he was three months old, however, he was well trained to lead and tie.

Riding Veggie to check cows, with my cow book in hand.

Our vet gelded him for us at four months, since this surgery is always easier when colts are young and still have mama for comfort and exercise. A foal usually gets plenty of exercise out in a pasture following mom around; there's very little aftercare involved when gelding a colt at that age. But Veggie developed a lot of swelling and we had to open the incisions again for better drainage —and he didn't appreciate that. I led him around the pasture for exercise to help the swelling go down, leading him from his mama, trotting around and around the pasture.

He was a fidget-fusser with lots of nervous energy, and quite a mama's boy, so we thought weaning might be traumatic for him. We decided to try "fenceline" weaning, which was starting to be recognized as the least stressful weaning method. We put Khamir and Veggie in one of the calving pens for a few days until Veggie felt at home there, then moved Khamir into the adjacent pen.

They still had each other for company, right through the fence, and Veggie wasn't too worried. We left them in those pens for a week, until he was fully weaned, then took her away. He ran and screamed for a few hours and then settled down and accepted the situation, since he still had horses nearby for company.

He lived in that pen through winter, but became bored because of his hyper nature, with nothing to do. I handled him a lot but since I was the only novelty in his boring day, he became pushy. It was getting harder to keep him well mannered. I put him with Surrocco for the rest of the winter and the 13-year-old gelding taught him more manners and respect in a short time than I could have done in a long time. He soon realized he wasn't the boss. This made my training job easier! He lived with Surrocco for a year, until I put him with his younger half-sister Rubbie, after she was weaned, and they lived together (most of the time) from then on.

He and Rubbie have been like soul mates their whole lives. He's now 28 years old and she's 27. They are similar, since they have the same sire, and their mothers were closely related (they are more than half siblings) but also very different. Veggie is tall, long-backed, long-necked and long-legged. He's long-striding, with fast walk and eager-beaver travel habits, always wanting to go fast. He has less than ideal conformation for anything but smooth, fast travel; his neck is a bit upside-down and hooked in too low on his shoulder and it's difficult for him to truly collect and get his hindquarters underneath himself for agile cow work or going downhill gracefully.

Veggie was never as agile as Rubbie. He could never jump freely; he tripped over logs and floundered through ditches and bogs. He has a much faster walk and trot than she does, but also

Veggie

Emily on Veggie, riding with her mom on Breezy in 2006.

threw back to gaited tendencies on his mama's side of the family. His mama Khamir and grandmother Khamette were true trotters but Khamette's mother Scrappy did a singlefoot (and could not trot), and Scrappy's mother was a pacer. When Veg walks really fast he shifts into a four-beat broken pace which is very smooth but has a lot of side-to-side motion.

By contrast, Rubbie took after the Arab and Quarter horse in her background; she is more compact, very short backed, and post-legged (she got her hind leg conformation from the Quarter Horse) which has been hard on her stifle joints and they've gone bad in her older years. Rubbie has the ability to collect and change direction quickly and smoothly. But she can't walk or trot as fast as Veggie; she has to jog or gallop to keep up with his walk or trot. Also they have very different back conformation. Veggie has great withers and a saddle never turns (even if the cinch is loose) nor slides forward going downhill. Rubbie's withers are lower than her rump (thanks to those jacked up hind legs with too-straight stifles!) and the saddle is constantly sliding forward if we're going downhill. But she was much more agile than Veggie galloping downhill after a cow, and more agile than her mama on the downhill chases.

Veggie was never the best cowhorse, but a fun horse to ride if you needed to trot over the range in a hurry to check gates and fences. I did manage to move a lot of cows with him, however. And there were a few times I was riding by myself and had to move groups of cows into the next range pasture, and make sure they were pairs, sorting back any cows or calves that didn't have their other half. Veggie and I could do it ok (even though we didn't have another rider to guard the gate), but it just took a lot of patience and slow cattle handling and planning ahead on our strategy. We couldn't do any fancy sorting so we relied on patient slow movement and a lot of cow psychology.

He was so goofy and hyper that I never thought he'd be a safe kid horse. He was spooky and silly, frantic if he got very far away from his buddies (especially if Rubbie was going a different direction – he was really married to her) and he was always trying to hurry too fast on the way home. But when Andrea's oldest daughter Emily was seven and wanted to learn to ride a horse, he was the only option available. By that time Veggie was 19 and had mellowed a bit.

I started taking her on short rides that fall, leading Veggie from Rubbie. This gave Emily a chance to learn how to handle the reins for stopping and turning, and practice trying to control him (keep him down to a dull roar when he wanted to go too fast) but grandma had the lead rope and could add more control when needed. That way we could ride side-by-side and I could keep Veggie at the same speed as Rubbie, and not let him get going too fast.

Emily did very well with her riding lessons. I started her the next spring, leading again, and we went over the low range on Veggie and Rubbie and extended our rides. There are several places where snow melt collects in the spring, making ponds. When those dry up, they are flat grassy areas, bigger than an arena, and probably the only truly flat and level areas on our range. We'd ride to one of those and I'd sit on Rubbie in the middle and let Emily practice walking and trotting Veggie solo in circles around me in the dry "ponds." She gained confidence in her ability to direct and control him, and was soon able to ride him solo all the time without me leading him.

By mid-summer she sometimes went with me to ride range. Veg began to settle down even more as he bonded with Emily, and an amazing thing happened. He decided he liked being a kid horse and started responding to her very nicely rather than just trying to go too fast or run back to Rubbie if we had to separate.

On one of our rides through the high range, we found a stray bull and a few cows from the neighboring range. Emily helped me herd them down the draw toward a little gate. I wasn't sure if we could get them through the gate because Veggie gets upset if he's far from the other horse, and we needed to split up. But Em was game to try, so we rode down and I opened the gate, then positioned her and Veggie on the edge of the timber, back from the gate. I told her to keep him calm and quiet and wait there, and make sure the cattle didn't run past the gate and into the timber.

I rode slowly and quietly up around the cattle to ease them down toward the gate, without them getting all spooky and trying to run off. Veggie whinnied at Rubbie a couple times (and she screamed back at him, because she's always been just as silly about being separated), but Em talked to him quietly and petted his neck and told him what a good boy he was. Amazingly he listened to her and stood still – not trying to prance around and run back to my horse. He'd become quite fond of that little kid, and took good care of her when she was riding him.

She and Veg guarded the escape direction and when I brought the cows down toward the gate they hesitated at the sight of the horse standing there and didn't try to run into the timber. While pausing there, they finally saw the gate and went through it. We followed them down into their range to join them up with some other cattle, and Em was proud of her accomplishment at being able to help move cows.

The next summer when Em was nine she rode with me a lot to check fences, gates and troughs and found a couple of elk horns. In late summer someone vandalized most of the troughs on our high range, slicing the plastic pipes that brought water into the troughs or taking them apart at the elbows. She helped me fix them all. She also rode Veggie several times with her older cousins (Heather and Nick) and Michael and Carolyn when we helped them move cows.

When we were gathering all the cows off the middle range pasture and moving them to the high range, we all split up to gather cattle from different areas. It was terribly windy that day, and we were hanging onto our hats. Emily and Nick went with

Riding Rubbie and leading Veggie with Dani aboard.

me to gather cattle from a series of ridges. At one point we were behind a ridge that blocked the wind, but when we came around the other side, the wind hit us full force. The horses didn't want to face into it. I grabbed my hat before it blew away, and the wind blew my hair in all directions. Nick and Em laughed at my appearance and called me an "electric" grandma. Veg was nervous in the wind but Em handled him ok on that steep slope and we followed our little group of cows around to the high range gate. Veg had transitioned nicely into being a dependable horse for Emily.

When Em's younger siblings started riding (at a younger age than she did), Veg was the one they started on, led from my horse. I could take a grandkid along on Veg if I was riding Rubbie. Those old horses were a harmonious team and Veg would behave himself. I could lead him alongside Rubbie, or have him drop behind on a narrow trail – just like I did with his grandmother Khamette when my kids were learning to ride.

When Samantha started riding Veg, she bonded with him, just like Em did. They got along great and he would behave nicely for her. She was the only one who rode him the last three years of his ridden career; Emily graduated to one of our new horses. Even though Veg was old and stiff and stumbled, Sam didn't mind. She was always well balanced and "rode it out" whenever he tripped and fell – sometimes clear down on his knees – and never fell off. He actually stumbled less frequently with a child riding him (light rider, light saddle) than when carrying a heavier adult and a big saddle.

Finally his stifle joints became arthritic and he wasn't sound enough to be ridden. As of this year, 2014, he and Rubbie became fully retired. His teeth are bad. Although we've had them floated it's hard for him to eat hay. Three years ago he got thin and Rubbie got fat, since she ate more of the hay. Even though Veg was always the boss, and sometimes chased her away from his hay, he was a picky eater and when he'd quit for a while she finished his hay for him. For the last two winters we had to keep them separate so he would get enough to eat. We moved him to another pen, but neither one of them was happy because he was on the other side of the barnyard. This past winter we simply split their old pen with an electric fence, with him on one side and her on the other. That way he was still next to her, but he could take all day to eat his hay, and get enough to eat.

Now, however, her teeth are bad, too. She's starting to show her age and was losing weight this spring. In her younger years I never grazed them at pasture because she was such an easy

Veggie

Andrea leading Veggie as a foal.

keeper she would be too fat (and possibly founder) if she had all the grass she wanted. Now that's changed, and this summer they were at pasture together and fully enjoying their retirement. Those two are so bonded that if something ever happens to one of them the other would probably die of a broken heart.

THE MUPPETS
Miss Piggy, Kermit and Fozzy

The first summer we kept Heidi's junior stallion here (a son of Surrabu) we bred two mares – Katy and Khamir. When Heidi brought him, she also brought me a young Arabian mare she'd already bred to him, so we were expecting three foals the next year. The young mare had a fancy name but we called her Pumpkin because of her golden pumpkin color. I started training her and rode her a little that summer while she was in early pregnancy. She was nice to work with and handle, and easy to start under saddle, but terribly clumsy. I hoped her foal would be more agile!

Our old calving pens by the house were falling apart and not very safe anymore for horses, so early that next spring (1990) we rebuilt them, making them more horse-proof (taller fence, V-mesh netting a horse can't put a foot through, chicken wire wrapped around the posts and top pole so a horse can't chew them). Pumpkin gave birth to her foal in one of the new pens. He was a cute little guy, with hind legs a little like a frog, so I named him Kermit. He was very friendly and people-oriented.

Katy foaled next – a good-looking bay filly we named Miss Piggy. She was standoffish, stubborn and independent from the moment she was born. Khamir foaled a few weeks later – a chestnut colt. He had lax tendons at first (hind fetlock joints down on the ground) but straightened up in a few days. Andrea named him Fozzy. Those were our Muppets.

They were very different. Kermit continued to be friendly, eager to be with people. Miss Piggy continued to be independent and did *not* want to be caught. We had to corner her between her mama and the fence. Fozzy started out mellow and friendly, and became more independent as he grew older.

Kermit and Fozzy were easy to halter train and lead and tie up, but Miss Piggy fought every time. Next to Sadie, she was the most challenging youngster I've ever raised. With Miss Piggy I had the advantage of handling her from birth, but that didn't seem to matter. Kermit and Fozzy only needed a butt rope a few times to encourage them to lead, but Miss Piggy always hung back on the rope unless we had the rear "come along". She set back every time I tied her up, and I'd stand behind her to make sure she didn't pull back too hard and hurt her neck.

The boys were easy to catch, but Miss Piggy continued her stubborn ways, and as a weanling I had to leave a halter on her, dragging a rope in her pen. At least the new foaling/weaning pens were safe, with nothing for a halter and rope to catch on. The boys spent their first winter together in a large pen, but I kept Miss Piggy in the small pen because she'd be uncatchable in the big one. She couldn't run far in the small pen, and with the trailing rope I could casually walk through the pen and pick it up, and she was caught. Eventually she realized the futility of being elusive, and by the time she was a yearling she no longer needed the halter; I could walk up and catch her.

When they were yearlings, the three of them got lots of leading lessons, but Miss Piggy was the most reluctant pupil. As two-year-olds we led them farther afield. Andrea led Fozzy on long walks on the jeep road over the hill to the low range. By that time he didn't try to pull away from her and take off like he tried one time in the barnyard. Sometimes we'd lead him and Kermit together. Kermit was the most insecure.

Miss Piggy was a nice-looking filly with great athletic potential (the most agile of the three) but was going to take a lot of work. We sold her, and her older brother Brumby (who I'd already started under saddle), to a lady and her daughter in Montana.

Andrea and I concentrated on training Kermit and Fozzy. Andrea led Fozzy many miles over the low range, and one day when she was two miles from home, she decided they'd done enough ground work. She simply got on him over there and rode him home. From then on she just kept riding him.

Kermit was more insecure. For his first rides out of the pen, Andrea walked beside us as I rode him, and gave him emotional support if things got too scary for him. She could snap a lead line onto his halter if he panicked. After he was more stable in his reactions to the big wide world, he and I tagged along with Andrea riding range when she was riding an older horse.

He was always insecure, especially that first year. If we had to separate from the other horse he'd scream and jump. It took a couple years before he was very manageable and could keep his wits about him when we had a job to do by ourselves.

Kermit as a weanling.

Fozzy was more independent. Andrea could ride him out by himself with no problems, but he sometimes tested her. He was also a challenge to shoe. He had a front foot that was becoming more upright by the time he was two and I had to keep it trimmed diligently to keep it from becoming a club foot. He also tended to interfere, and with shoes he sometimes struck the opposite fetlock joint. I had to shoe him very carefully.

He was kind of a stinker to shoe, and one summer we had a professional farrier shoe him a couple times, but Fozzy interfered severely with those shoes – so I went back to shoeing him myself. He had a hitch in his stride from the uneven hoof angles because his shoulders were uneven, but with careful shoeing I could keep it to a minimum.

When he was still green, Andrea was helping me move cattle up through the creek canyon on the high range, and ran into some

237

old wire that had been part of a power line to the old Harmony Mine (abandoned in the 1930s). Fozzy had loops of wire clear up past his hocks. He just stopped, and Andrea was able to keep him calm until I got there to hold him while Andrea carefully picked his feet up and got his legs out of the wire.

The summer of 1994, when he was four, she was still riding him in a snaffle, but that changed after an episode when we were coming home through the 320 from the high range after a day of checking cows. Andrea and Fozzy were ahead of me and my horse. He bumped a rock with a hind foot and it rolled down the hill and passed him--and spooked him--and he instantly bucked and the saddle started turning (the cinch was loose because she'd run out of holes). Andrea rode it out for a few jumps, but he was going downhill and had his head down pretty good and bucked her off. She landed hard on her shoulder. This was just two weeks before her wedding to Jim and I envisioned her in a body cast for the wedding! But she was just scraped and bruised.

Fozzy didn't run off; he came back to her, and she got on again and we continued home. But after that she got a shorter cinch, and put curb reins on the Pelham bit and rode him with a curb as well as a snaffle, to have more control if he tried to put his head down to buck. He had a short strong neck, like his sire, and it was hard to keep his head up if he really wanted to drop it down. He never bucked her off again, but there were a couple times he tried, when he was angry.

One memorable time was when we were coming down from the high range in the rain, bringing a cow home that needed doctored. We'd gotten her down through the brushy canyon and were bringing her down the road to a corral on our upper place.

Andrea and Fozzy riding range.

I trotted ahead to open the gate and Andrea was bringing the cow with Fozzy. He was so mad because we'd gone on ahead, and mad because the rain was hitting him in the face. He didn't see any purpose in following that cow.

He tried to bolt but she wouldn't let him. So he tried to buck and she wouldn't let him. So he reared up and literally ran down the road on his hind legs for about 150 yards. It was the weirdest sight, and she said it was the weirdest sensation, riding a rearing, running horse! Like the Lippizan horses that do "airs above the ground," jumping on their hind legs, he must have had incredibly strong hindquarters! She leaned forward as much as possible (tight against his neck) so as not to pull him over backward, yet not let him have his head enough to buck, and he kept running forward with his front legs up in the air before he came back down to earth.

As time went on, however, he became more of a team player and Andrea really enjoyed riding him. He was a challenge, but a tough horse – like Surrocco – with a high pain tolerance and lots of endurance. He and Kermit were both progressing in their usefulness and abilities, and then I lost Kermit.

We'd had a good summer and he was finally becoming a good ranch horse. We had the cattle gathered that fall and the horses were enjoying a bit of time off. Kermit colicked one cold, rainy evening. We gave him Banamine and put him in the barn out of the wind and rain, but he didn't improve.

I was really sick that day, too, with a stomach bug and severe headache, and wasn't able to be with him very much; Andrea and Lynn stayed out in the barn with Kermit and kept walking him and treating him for pain. But nothing helped. We had the vet out, but it was hopeless, and we put him down. Within less than 24 hours I'd lost my silly Kermit frog – the friendly guy with the timid heart.

Fozzy took his place as my choretime alarm clock. Kermit had always whinnied if I wasn't out there at exactly the proper time (you could set your watch by him), and after he was gone, Fozzy started doing the same thing.

Fozzy continued to be a good horse for Andrea, and she rode him lots of miles checking cows and moving cows – even though he didn't like cows. When he was still green, he'd jump backward if they swatted their tails in his face. If he had to keep following them he'd get mad and start biting them.

He was also notorious for his explosive kick. If something startled him from the rear he'd kick first and ask questions later. He never kicked a person, but we made sure we didn't come

Andrea checking cows on Fozzy.

up behind him without his knowing we were there! One day when Andrea was ahead of me on the trail, Fozzy walked past a rattlesnake and it struck at his hind leg. He kicked it in mid-strike and it never hit him. Watching it happen, I was amazed at how quickly he whammed that snake!

Andrea rode him to alternate with Breezy (a Morgan mare) for all her range riding, until her burn accident when Fozzy was 10 years old. After that, there were several years she didn't ride much at all and I didn't want her to try to ride him again because she wasn't very strong and he might have dumped her. She was just too fragile to risk it. By the time she might have been able to ride him again, he wasn't sound anymore. His front foot had continued to become more upright because I hadn't been shoeing him or keeping his feet trimmed as often as they needed. His club foot had become worse--so he was basically retired.

Andrea still "visited" him and they shared a special bond, and we kept him until his age and infirmities made it necessary to put him down. He and Snickers were both in failing health by last fall (2013). Snickers was getting senile and losing her vision, and Fozzy had tumorous growths under his flanks, so we put them down before winter.

Michael helped with this unpleasant task, and dug a grave for the two of them with our backhoe in a shady spot across the creek behind the haystack. Andrea led Fozzy out of his pen, across the bridge and over to the stackyard. She sat on a bale of hay and talked with him a few moments to say good-by as he grazed. As she led him over there, through the barnyard, his crippled condition was painfully obvious. But he'd had a good life, and the fact he was still perky and happy was a tribute to his toughness and resilience and resistance to pain.

BREEZY
Cow Chases, Colic and a Cancer Comeback

In 1996 we were looking for a horse for Andrea's husband Jim. We'd tried out an Arabian the year before – a gray gelding named Nothing Major – that came from Oregon. Several of us rode him that summer. He was a kind, willing horse, but had a knee problem (from a growth that had been surgically removed the year before) and wasn't completely sound. The former owner took him back.

So we went to look at a young Morgan mare (born in August 1991) raised and trained here in our valley. She was a dark liver chestnut named Carmen Willow Breeze. Breezy, as we called her, was started under saddle but still green. She was hyper and nervous, but an eager traveler, and we decided to buy her.

Not long after we got her, however, she colicked. Our vet came out to administer tranquilizer and mineral oil. We thought she might have eaten some strange plants/weeds in the woodsy area of her pen that was across the creek, so we put an electric fence along this side to keep her from going over there.

243

She continued to have mild colic episodes periodically (never as bad as that first one), but enough that we began to wonder if she had a gut problem. We learned later that several of her half-siblings had chronic colic problems and a couple of them had died of colic, so we wondered if there might be a genetic tendency.

Breezy often had mild indigestion. She'd stretch a lot, perhaps from gas pains. If it got worse, she'd paw, and lie down. My sister suggested feeding her yeast daily, to possibly help her digestion. Thus began a daily chore, mixing a heaping tablespoon of yeast in cold water and squirting it by syringe into her mouth, at morning feeding. At first she didn't like it (she was also difficult to deworm by oral dose syringe) and Lynn helped me every morning, holding her for me and twisting her upper lip (hand twitch) so she'd stand still and not flip her head to avoid it.

After a few weeks, she got so used to the procedure that it was easy to give her yeast every morning as part of our daily routine. It did seem to help. She occasionally had mild discomfort and stretching episodes (mostly in the fall and spring) but never again such severe colic. As time went on there also seemed to be a pattern to some of the stretching episodes; if she got really upset or excited (after a wild cow chase, or if there were lots of strange horses along on a cattle drive and she was very hyper) she was more likely to have a mild colic.

The first summer we had her, Jim rode her some, but Andrea rode her a lot, trading off between Breezy and Snickers. The next couple of years, Snickers was becoming stiff in the knees from all the hard miles, so Andrea rode Breezy more and more. Before long, Snickers was semi-retired.

Breezy

Breezy

Andrea and Breezy riding range with Carolyn in 1999.

Breezy became a really good cowhorse, taking Snickers place as Andrea's main range-riding horse. When Jim and Andrea split up several years later, Jim gave her to Andrea. Breezy was fun to ride because she liked to go, and had a fast trot. Even if she was sometimes clumsy and tripped at a walk, if she was trotting she could really fly, and always picked her feet up (typical Morgan leg action) and never missed her footing. She could fly down a hill after a wayward cow and head her off, every time.

Andrea loved riding her almost as much as Snickers. She was riding Breezy on the 4th of July, 2000, the last day that she and I rode together before her burn injury the night of July 5. We were searching for and rounding up five cows off the range – the cows that had young bull calves that we planned to keep as bulls. We wanted to bring them home, before they got any older and became too precocious and tried to breed cows. It was a wild ride because the cows and their bull calves didn't want to come home, and led us on some merry chases. But Rubbie and Breezy did a great job and we got them.

Then, our lives changed forever. Andrea was visiting friends on the other side of the mountain, the evening of July 5, and they set off fireworks. The family dog tried to grab a rocket as it took off, deflecting it toward the sagebrush-covered mountain behind the house rather than straight up in the sky. It hit the tall, dry sagebrush and immediately started a fire. Andrea called the fire department. Her friend Mark started his crawler tractor and headed up there to try to create a fire line to contain the fire before it went on up the mountain, and Andrea went with him to try to help.

A wind came up, and the fire exploded and grew before they could get far, then the wind brought it raging up the hill toward them. The hill was too steep to outrun it with the crawler tractor, so Mark put it in neutral and let it roll back down the hill, through the flames, to an area that had already burned, where it would be safe to jump off and run. Andrea panicked as the crawler tractor careened backward down the hill, bouncing and almost tipping over, and she jumped off – right into the 30-foot high flames – and ran through them to get away from the fire. Mark spun the crawler around sideways to stop it after it got through the flames, then jumped off to find her. They ran down a draw to the house, where the fire crew found them and took them by ambulance 12 miles to our hospital and then life-flighted them to the Intermountain Burn Center in Salt Lake City.

Andrea spent the rest of that summer in the ICU fighting for her life, undergoing skin graft surgeries and then as an outpatient

Andrea after her burn, giving Emily a short ride on Breezy in 2002.

having wounds dressed and bandaged daily, until she could come home in September. Family members took turns being with her in the ICU, and Lynn stayed through her outpatient stint at my cousin's home nearby. I stayed here at the ranch to take care of her two-and-a-half-year-old daughter Emily, and trying to take care of the ranch. Friends and neighbors helped with haying and range riding.

After her burn injuries (hands, arms, and legs – with some deep fourth-degree burns, down into the muscles and tendons on her legs) Andrea could barely walk, but she'd worked hard at her physical therapy. The day she got home she accomplished two goals. She wanted to be able to lift her little daughter again, and she wanted to be able to walk out into the barnyard far enough to see her horses.

She wasn't able to ride for nearly a year after her accident, but got on a horse briefly the next spring. She rode Breezy on a couple of very short rides that summer of 2001. She rode Breezy again in 2003 for one short ride when a photographer was here taking pictures of the whole family (Lynn, me, Michael and Carolyn and their two kids, and Andrea) on horseback. But she didn't start riding again for real until several years later, after she'd had her other children, and her arms and legs were stronger again.

Breezy had basically been on vacation for six years while Andrea was recovering, regaining her life and strength. Andrea started riding her again in 2006, a few short rides with me and Emily (who was eight years old and riding Veggie by then). In late June Andrea came out to the ranch to ride with us and it was a very special occasion with three generations of cowgirls riding together! It was great to see Andrea riding her high spirited mare again, with all her former confidence.

I told Emily that Andrea and I used to do a lot of range riding together and that sometimes we'd take our lunch, on long rides. Emily wanted to do that, so three weeks later we three girls rode again – on Veggie, Breezy and Rubbie – and had a picnic lunch up Baker Creek in the 320, in a grassy meadow. We ate our sandwiches in the shade of aspen trees while our horses grazed in the meadow.

Then we made a loop through the range pastures and checked water troughs. We cleaned out a springbox that wasn't working very well and found four frogs in it. Em really wanted those frogs, so we ate the last muffin in our lunch bag and brought those frogs home in the plastic bag – with a little water in it. Andrea carried the bag of frogs all the way home on Breezy.

Breezy

Samantha, age 11, riding Breezy in 2014 after Breezy's eye removal.

The next summer Andrea rode Breezy a little more, and helped me move cows several times, and helped us round up Michael and Carolyn's cows off the upper 160-acre and 320-acre mountain pastures in the fall. The next year, 2010, she rode so regularly that I finally had to put shoes on Breezy again, for the first time in 10 years! Her feet are strong and hard, and she managed without shoes for all the sporadic rides before that.

Andrea and Breezy eventually picked up where they left off, chasing cows, riding range to check gates and fences. Then three years ago when Breezy was 20, we bought a younger horse that Andrea has been riding and training, and her kids started riding Breezy. Em rode her a lot during the summer of 2012, helping me ride range. Then last year Samantha started riding her a few times, transitioning from old Veggie, who was 27 years old by then and starting to stumble more often.

Sam got along pretty well with Breezy and was able to keep her from going too fast when she's feeling hyper, and it looked like Breezy would make a good horse for her. We were hoping that Breezy and Sam can be a good team for a few years until Spotty Dottie (a Morgan filly I'm training) is well trained enough to become a mount for Sam.

Then we noticed a growth on Breezy's left eye. She's always had a lot of sclera (the white part of the eye) showing in the back corners of her eyes, and as she grew older these areas suffered irritation from sunlight, flies and dust. The smooth white tissue became rough and reddened, so we had a vet look at her eyes. He said they were simply irritated. No cancer. So we just kept monitoring her eyes.

Then late last fall (when she was 22) her left eye showed more bumpiness and extra tissue starting to grow over the edge of her cornea. We had another vet look at it and take a biopsy. Cancer. Since it was on the surface of the eye itself, and the vet was unsure how deep it went, her recommendation was to either monitor it and put the mare down when it became a quality-of-life issue as the cancer spread, or remove the eye and hope that the cancer had not yet spread beyond the eyeball. We opted for surgery, to try to give Breezy more good years. Her surgery was scheduled for the end of December.

In planning for this major event, we helped Breezy get used to what it would be like to be sightless on that side. Carolyn sewed a couple layers of denim onto an old fly mask, covering the left side of her face. Breezy wore that for several weeks. We also borrowed Michael and Carolyn's trailer and parked it here to give her some practice getting in and out of the trailer (since she hadn't been in a trailer since she arrived at our ranch as a four-year-old). We got her used to getting in and out with that eye covered, and loaded her with Ed, her old buddy who is a veteran trailer traveler.

We hauled Breezy to the clinic on a cold day the end of December (with Ed riding along with her for emotional security), where our vet removed the eye. As soon as she was out from under the anesthesia and back on her feet and stable enough to walk, we loaded her back up with Ed (who had spent a couple hours in a corral behind the clinic), putting the padded fly mask over the bandage for protection and warmth. Weather was cold and stormy so we left it on her. We had tried to get her used to being in a barn (our calving barn) with another horse for company – before the surgery – but she was too nervous and upset in there so we knew she'd be happier out in her pen where she felt more comfortable, and knew her way around with one eye.

During the following weeks we changed the bandage until the sutured area quit oozing, keeping that side of her face covered/ padded and protected from cold weather with the padded fly mask. The first two weeks were miserable for her and we kept her on Banamine (to help with pain and inflammation) and antibiotics for about 10 days. By then she was doing much better.

It was fully healed by spring, and Andrea started riding her, to see if Breezy could manage with one eye. I rode with her. Breezy was totally comfortable as long as the other horse was on her good side where she could see us. She was at ease on all the trails and managed ok traveling over the rugged hillsides. Her rider just has to be careful to not get too close to brush/trees or a drop-off on her blind side.

Now my granddaughter Sam (age 11) is riding the mare again and they are doing fine. Sam is learning to be more conscientious, trying to be her "seeing eye" person on that side when leading or riding her. To watch them trotting around a mountainside or following cows, you'd never know the mare has only one eye. And Breezy now wears a fly mask all the time in her pen – to protect her good eye from sunlight in hopes that it won't develop cancer, too.

A MARE NAMED ED
And Other Characters

A few years after Michael and Carolyn came back to the ranch they needed another horse. They bought a little bay mare with blaze face, about 12 years old. The rancher who sold her wanted a larger, calmer horse. This mare is small (14.3 hands) and we don't know her breeding, but looks like she might be an Arab/Quarter Horse cross. She's heavier muscled than most Arabs but lighter muscled than a Quarter Horse, and has more endurance. She has a unique, quirky personality but is basically a "people horse" and easy to handle. Michael named her Ed but she has many nicknames – Eddie, Eddie Girl, Edwina, Edgarita, EddyAnn, etc.

Michael, Carolyn and their kids used her for several years as an all-purpose ranch horse, and then she was injured. She either got kicked on the hock, or pulled it badly in a fence or a bog. Her hock was huge and she was very lame. They didn't use her for two years. She gradually regained soundness but still has big hock.

HORSE TALES

I helped them move cattle a few times when they had to trailer their horses up the creek a long ways or to one of their leased places, and they'd take Ed along for me to ride since none of our current horses were trailer-trained. We don't own a trailer.

One spring she suddenly had a droopy lip (and her tongue protruded out that side of her mouth a little) and she had trouble eating (chewing more slowly, and dropping wads of hay or grass out that side of her mouth). They brought her and a couple other horses to our ranch to graze in our barnyard. After they took the other horses back to their place they left Ed here and loaned her to me, since my best cowhorse (Rubbie) was getting too old and stiff for long, hard rides. By then I was only using Rubbie when taking the grandkids on short rides with Veggie.

Ed's lip/tongue remained droopy for about a year. I suspected she'd been kicked or ran into something and injured a nerve on that side of her face and it just took a while to heal. Some years earlier we'd had a cow with similar facial paralysis on one side. Ed was able to eat, but had trouble drinking unless the water was deep enough that she could dunk her face into it clear past the corners of her mouth; otherwise she had no suction because she couldn't keep her lips closed. She'd stick her head halfway down into the water and blow bubbles. That winter I had to make sure there was enough water in her tub to be deep enough for her to drink, even though it meant getting more ice out of it the next morning. By spring her lip was less droopy and today it's hardly noticeable.

We made a trade (and I got Ed) so she continued to live at our place. I rode her fairly regularly, whenever we had to move or sort our cows, and helping Michael and Carolyn move their

Ed and me on the middle range pasture in 2013.

cattle. She was getting a bit stiff and not quite as agile as she used to be, but still more sound and agile than Rubbie.

She did a great job for me in September 2011 when Carolyn's brother and I helped Michael and Carolyn round up their cattle off the range, especially the day we had to find some of their cows that had gone to the wrong range – into the head of Mulkey Creek and Withington Creek. The fire in 2003 burned up several miles of fence between our range and the Forest allotment, and even though the fence was rebuilt, the burned dead trees that were still standing keep falling down, knocking over the fence, and the cattle can stray. They were short about 20 cows and two bulls so we'd split up to cover more country.

Carolyn's brother Brian and I found some of the cows up the right fork of Withington Creek, and as we were bringing them down I saw one of the bulls (a yearling named Freddy George)

255

with a group of the neighbor's cows which were departing swiftly over the hill. I left Brian bringing our group of cows, and Ed and I galloped up there and got the bull sorted off. But he didn't want to leave those cows, and kept trying to outrun us and go with them. Ed and I galloped down that steep hill, pushing that bull, and had to keep heading him off as he tried to evade us and go back to the departing cows.

Ed gave it her best try and we kept outrunning that bull and turning him. I had two sweatshirts tied behind my saddle and lost them somewhere on that mountainside as we ran down it full speed, ramming into that bull every time he tried to turn through us, but I was thankful Ed never lost her footing. Brian held his breath as that old mare and this old grandma went racing down that rocky mountainside full speed chasing that bull, but we got the job done.

By 2012 Andrea's younger kids were needing dependable horses to ride, besides old Veggie (who was 26), so we bought a six-year-old Quarter Horse mare at the Salmon Horse Sale. She was mellow and seemed like a good candidate. We nicknamed her Sprout. She was lazy and slow, but when we put a child on her she tried to run home or buck. Fortunately Andrea's youngest girl Danielle (age seven that year), who was riding her those times, stayed on, and we were able to grab the mare. Sprout had a few more bad habits that came to the surface, so Andrea and I took over riding and re-training her. We used her to ride range and put a lot of miles on her, and she started to learn about cows.

Sprout also had to learn about being nicer when her feet were handled for cleaning, trimming and shoeing. She interfered, hitting her right hind fetlock joint, making it bloody, so we had to use shin boots on her hind legs that first summer, to protect them. She had

*Me on Dottie (three-year-old in training),
grandkids on Ed & Breezy – October 2013.*

to learn to tolerate having those boots put on every time we rode.

Then she went lame on her left hind foot and we thought it was a stone bruise. We found a tender area in the middle of her frog, so we cut the frog away at that spot and it oozed a little. We soaked it and it got a little better, then she went lame again. We treated it, soaked and wrapped it (to keep dirt out of the hole under her frog) the rest of the summer and into the fall.

One day when we were cleaning up her foot and changing the bandage/wrap, some more frog shed off and we discovered an inch-long greasewood thorn down in there! That's why it wouldn't heal. So we got that out, and soaked the foot some more, and her lameness cleared up.

We protected her foot with a homemade boot until the tissue under the frog toughened up, and by then it was winter. The good thing about her lameness was that all the foot handling made her more tolerant about foot care, and she became a lot easier to shoe.

Over winter that mare grew. She was tall when we got her as a six year old, but a little thin, and after we'd had her a year she'd grown another inch and put on 200 pounds and had a bigger attitude, to match. When Andrea started riding her that next spring after her long vacation, Sprout was a nasty witch. She was hell-bent to have her own way, and tried to buck Andrea off every day, for more than a month. She finally realized that Andrea was in control, and quit trying – and became a team player. By summer's end she was a pretty good horse, and well bonded to Andrea, but still selfishly independent.

Realizing that Sprout wasn't going to make a kid horse any time soon, with her attitude, I bought a couple of Morgan fillies that fall – a chestnut weanling we named Willow (to raise and train for Dani) and a two-year-old palomino that I would train for Sam. The plan is for Sam and grandma to share that filly. Sam named her Spotty Dottie because of her dappled coat.

So, while Willow and Dottie are growing up and in training, the girls graduated to riding Ed and Breezy. Dani started riding Ed a lot last year (2013) when she was eight and the mare 20-something, to help grandma ride range and check range cows. She and Ed get along nicely. Dani is very proud to be able to chase cows with grandma. Andrea was gone for several weeks last summer, and Dani was my right-hand cowgirl helping move cows and check water troughs and fences. When I started riding Dottie (who was three by then) later in the summer, Dani rode along with me on Ed as my "baby sitter horse."

This year, at age nine, Dani is even more confident, and she and Ed are a good team. She catches and brushes Ed, cleans

Me on Dottie and nine-year-old Dani riding Ed to check the range, 2014.

her feet, saddles and bridles her, and loves to ride her bareback around the barnyard with just a halter on when she's putting her back in her pen after a ride. I hope Ed goes on quite a long time and can continue to be a good cowhorse for Dani until Willow grows up!

MOLLY AND CHANCE
Part of the Family

Horses often become part of the family – especially ranch horses that have spent their whole lives being part of the "team" and doing their best with any job they are asked to do. In the fall of 2013, our family had the sad task of putting down 4 elderly horses who had served us loyally for many years.

The oldest was Molly, at 31. This mare was raised by my daughter-in-law Carolyn when she was still in high school. Her family had Angus cattle and horses near Arco, Idaho. The foal was planned to be Carolyn's. The dam was a black Quarter Horse mare named Sally that Carolyn rode as a 4-H project. Sally was bred to a Morgan.

Sally was very protective of her newborn foals for a couple weeks and aggressive toward people before she foaled. They had to just turn her out in a field and leave her alone. She'd had several foals already, including Comanche, an older gelding.

Molly was born April 17, 1982. She was a light chestnut (and turned darker). Carolyn tried to think of a name and her dad said to not worry, that the foal would name itself. When they finally got close enough to see what sex the foal was, they caught her, and started some leading lessons. Her dad said, "Come on, Miss Molly Brown" and that name stuck.

Carolyn worked with the foal all the time, and did everything she could think of with Molly. "We never rode our horses until they were three. Dad never wanted me to climb on them the first time; my older brother Brian broke all our young horses. Brian climbed on Molly, rode her in the round pen for about 20 minutes and then got off and said, 'I don't have to break her. She's yours. Just get on and go.' I'd put my little saddle on her (the one we used on our Shetland) from the time she was a yearling."

Carolyn kept putting bigger saddles on her as the filly grew. Molly was used to being saddled, and Carolyn ponied her everywhere, leading the filly from whatever horse she was riding. "She was my buddy, and never learned how to buck."

After Michael and Carolyn were married, they brought Molly and Comanche to our ranch on Withington Creek. That first summer on the creek, Carolyn rode Molly to help with range riding and cattle work. Molly had her first encounter with a bear when Carolyn, Andrea and I were riding up the creek to check cattle on our high range. We came around a corner and the horses were startled to see a young bear playing Tarzan, pulling chokecherry branches down to eat the fruit. The waving branches and gyrating bear were too much for Molly. She freaked out and tried to whirl and run. Finally the bear noticed the nervous horses and Molly jumping around--and took off. But from that point on Molly was afraid of bears.

She could smell them before anyone could see them. Nothing

much else bothered her. If she started snorting and dancing, the rider always knew there was a bear nearby. A few years later when Andrea's husband Jim was riding Molly to help check cattle, Molly started snorting and tossing her head as we came toward a meadow on our upper mountain pasture, and sure enough--farther down the trail – a bear took off out of the bushes. None of the other horses had sensed its presence.

Molly was a horse anyone could ride. She was also a calm, dependable influence for the young horses we were training. The first summer Carolyn was here, she often rode with me when I was training Veggie, a young gelding. He was nervous and skittish and Molly was a great "baby sitter" horse.

She also had patience with cattle. Molly loved cows and if you rode her into a herd of cattle the calves would walk up and smell her. She'd stand patiently as they sniffed around her, and some tried to nurse her!

Michael and Carolyn have two children (born in 1991 and 1993), and they learned to ride on Molly. When they came back to the ranch (after leasing ranches at Arco and Mackay) and young Heather was riding Molly, one of the heifers, Miss Piggy, liked to chew on Molly's tail. When we'd round up cows that drifted too low on the range and push them up the hill and over to Baker Creek, young Heather had to go first, ahead of the cattle, because the heifers were so in love with Molly. They'd follow Molly up the hill, with Miss Piggy chewing on her tail. It was sometimes hard to sort cows on Molly because they wanted to be next to her.

For a few years Michael and Carolyn both had city jobs, in Boise, Idaho, and rented a little place at Kuna (on the outskirts of Boise) where they kept their horses. While they were in Kuna

Carolyn giving young Heather a ride on Molly, and me on Veggie.

they had a couple different farriers shoe their horses. One of them trimmed Molly's feet too deeply, into the quick, on all four feet. She developed abscesses and was so lame she could hardly walk. Michael and Carolyn had to soak and treat her feet a couple times a day, and she was very patient when they were doing it out there in the dark – before and after work.

Michael started shoeing Molly himself after that. From that time on he did all their shoeing. After the bad experience with the farrier, it was difficult to even trim her feet until she learned to trust again. It was a slow and patient process. "When I first started trying to trim and shoe her, she was so upset and nervous that I had to clear my thoughts of all nervousness myself because she'd just fight me," recalls Michael. "If there were other people around I had to ask them to leave, so there were no distractions, no nervous vibes. Everything had to be calm. I had to approach it as if it would be just fine, and then it would be fine." Horses teach us a lot about patience and trust.

After Michael and Carolyn had their children, they decided they didn't want to live in the city. They rented Carolyn's mom's 80-acre place at Arco, and then leased a ranch near Mackay. Their kids started riding at a young age. They rode around in the pasture with Heather on Jon Boy (the Arab-Appaloosa gelding that Grandpa Don – my father – gave to Heather) and Nick rode in front of Carolyn on Molly. "We spent a lot of time doing that, with Nick learning how to hold the reins and steer. This is how Heather started learning to ride, sitting in the saddle in front of me," recalls Carolyn.

In the spring of 1999 their little family moved back here to our ranch and we built a house for them on our upper place. They leased the neighboring ranch for 11 years (the one Lynn and I had leased for 29 years) and several other ranches. That summer young Heather (age eight) and Nick (age six) rode Molly a lot. One of the first times Nick rode Molly solo we were moving cattle. Nick and Molly were bringing up the rear by themselves. Nick had to get off Molly to pee, and none of us were close enough to help monitor his horse. We worried about whether Molly would wait for him or try to go home, or if she'd stand still for him to climb back on. It was quite a feat for little Nick to pull himself high enough to get his foot in that short stirrup! But Molly stood patiently; she always took good care of the kids. She gave Nick confidence. She tolerated everything he did and he was never afraid of her.

That same summer, we were moving cows up a steep hill. Carolyn and young Heather were on the far side of the herd on

Yearling heifer sniffing Molly's tail.

their horses, and Nick was riding with me. I was riding a young horse and he was on Molly. His saddle started slipping back, as we went up the steep ridge. We weren't in a good place to stop, and with my inexperienced horse I wasn't able to get off right then to help him. So Nick just kept riding, with the saddle sliding back toward Molly's rump – the cinch almost to her flanks. But that mare didn't fuss and we made it safely to the top, where we could stop and reset his saddle.

The kids used to ride around their house nearly every day. Heather would catch Jon Boy, and if they worked together they could get a saddle up on him, and get it cinched. Heather could get a bridle on Jon Boy, but it was hard to get a bridle on Molly so Nick usually rode with just a halter.

One day they decided to go on a picnic with the horses, over the hill to a meadow. They took a lunch, the dogs and the horses.

They thought since they were on a picnic they should unsaddle the horses and let them graze. Jon Boy and Molly decided that since they were that close to home, they'd just go home. The kids came running home after them – and had to ride the horses bareback over the hill to go get their saddles.

That next summer the kids rode in the fields bareback to turn bales – turning any that ended up on their sides, so the stackwagon could pick them up. By then they were in 4-H with their horses, so they practiced figure-eights and other maneuvers around the bales. Nick was able to start 4-H when he was seven, and showed Molly that year. The next year they closed that program and he had to wait until he was nine to be in 4-H again.

During the year he couldn't be in 4-H, the kids did jackpot rodeo and Nick won several hundred dollars on Molly. She'd never barrel raced but would try anything. She wasn't very fast, but could maintain her speed around the barrels better than most horses, so Nick won a lot of barrel races.

Nick also did well in flag races. Molly could get close to the bucket and never slow down, and Nick was so agile and acrobatic that he could lean out and grab the flags and drop them in the next bucket at the other end of the arena. Nick trusted that mare so much that one time when he was practicing for the flag race he leaned over so far he fell off. Molly just stopped and waited for him to get back on.

Nick was always goofing around and playing imaginary sword games with sticks, even when riding Molly. Sometimes when he rode through trees or tall sagebrush, if Molly thought Nick was too busy with his sticks and wasn't paying enough attention, she would move over into the bush just enough to whack him (and get his attention) but not enough to hurt him or knock him off.

By the next year (2003), when Nick was nine and back in 4-H, Molly was 21 and slowing down, with arthritic joints. "We tried to breed her, and gave her a year off in hopes of having a foal. So that April at the horse sale we bought a middle-aged gelding for Nick, called Mr. K. Nick showed him in 4-H instead of Molly. Molly was too old, however, to have a foal," says Carolyn. Nick did well with Mr. K, and Molly was retired.

But she got pulled out of retirement for a tough job that summer (July 2003) when a forest fire threatened our range and cattle. Lightning started a fire on the mountain above our range. The Forest Service started dumping water by helicopter but the fire continued to grow. Michael and Carolyn rode that afternoon to try to gather all the cattle in the right fork of Withington Creek, in case the fire came that direction.

Carolyn rode Molly (even though she was fat and out of shape, with no shoes on) because she knew the range so well. "I'd ridden her many times up there in the dark, on long days moving cattle coming home in the dark. I felt most confident riding her. Michael was riding Chester, a young green horse. We knew it would be a hard, fast ride, and possibly getting home after dark. We gathered all the cattle out of the right fork canyon, to get them out of harm's way. I trusted Molly completely, because I'd ridden her so many years. She got me onto the trails and out of there safely even though it was pitch black bringing the cows down," recalls Carolyn.

For the next several days Michael and Carolyn rode daily to monitor the fire, looking across from the ridge between Baker Creek and Withington Creek, watching the fire on the mountain behind the head of Withington Creek. They planned to gather all their cattle on the Baker Creek side if the fire came their way. The Forest Service crews had pumper trucks filling water tanks for the helicopters, dumping water on the fire, but it continued to grow, moving toward Salmon.

Then the fire blew up. The wind brought it back toward our range and we had to hurriedly get the cows out of there. The 4-H horse show was in progress, and the kids had their horses at the fairgrounds so Carolyn had to use Molly again. Lynn drove up on the range with our jeep, opening all the gates. Michael and Carolyn galloped their horses several miles up the creek and into the Baker Creek drainage where they and their dogs hurriedly gathered cattle.

That day, as they were hurrying up Baker Creek and Michael split off to go over the ridge on the town side to gather cattle out of Basco Basin, Molly just flew. She could sense the urgency and gave it everything she had. She was a little tenderfooted without shoes, after the previous hard ride through rocky country a few evenings earlier, but she didn't hold back.

"She just continued to do the job, whatever I asked her to do. Coming down the rocky ridge following the cows after we finally had them gathered, I got off and led her part way because she was sore-footed, and let her catch her breath, because we knew there would be another hard push to bring the other cattle on down – the ones that we'd put into our upper pasture a few nights earlier. It's a good thing she had tough feet!" recalls Carolyn. They were able to get all the cows out, just ahead of the fire.

It was scary for awhile, with burning embers falling on them as the fire roared up the mountain out of Withington Creek, right to the ridge they were coming down with the cattle. It looked like they would be engulfed in flames. Then the wind changed direction as

Nick helping gather and move cows on Molly in spring 2000.

the fire reached the ridge and miraculously stopped before it cut off their escape route.

Molly was surefooted. "We could always trust her to find her footing, chasing cows. Michael was riding her on one of our leased places where there were thousands of badger holes, and had to gallop through there to head off cows, and she never stepped in any of those holes. She watched her footing," says Carolyn.

She had a lot of endurance. One of her longest hard rides was when Michael and Carolyn came up from Arco one fall to round up cattle. We rode all day for several days. On the next to last day, Andrea, Carolyn and I made a long ride, coming home at dark. Molly broke into a second sweat. Her muscles quivered as we started home but she recovered and went again the next morning.

She was always willing to do any job, but later in life was

269

hesitant to go through a bog, because she got bogged down so badly at one of their leased places. Michael was riding her to move cows and she got stuck in mud up past her belly. She stayed calm while he got off and then she fought her way out of it. She had to lunge and struggle, but tried not to crash into Michael. There were some old fences on that place, too, and if she got into a tangle of wire she didn't panic. She'd just stop and let her rider get off and get her feet untangled.

It was during the half dozen years that Michael was riding Molly as his main cowhorse that he realized he preferred riding mares over geldings. "She had so much endurance and heart, and would give you everything she had, and then some, when there was a tough job to do. She'd keep going even when she shouldn't. She was a versatile, all-around ranch horse. We packed fencing materials on her, salt, and game during hunting season. She was an incredible horse whether you were going full speed through a gopher colony to head a cow, or packing an elk. If she did stumble, she always caught herself and never fell down."

Molly's best buddy Chance was an Arabian gelding. He was 17 when he was given to my oldest granddaughter Heather by her great aunt (my sister) for Christmas in 2000, when Heather was nine. His registered name was Omega Chance and he was chestnut with white blaze and socks. Even though he was well into his teens he was still in his prime; he looked and acted like a much younger horse. He had the wisdom and manners of age, however, and was the perfect horse for a young girl.

Heather remembers that Christmas vividly. "Nick and I both had huge boxes under the tree. Nick opened his first, and it was

Granddaughter Heather and Chance guarding the gate while cows are sorted.

an English saddle. When I opened mine, it was a series of smaller and smaller boxes, and finally just an envelope – with Chance's registration papers. As I was unwrapping all those layers, I was disappointed because Nick had gotten a saddle, and my present just kept getting smaller until I came to that envelope. I thought it was just a joke, and then I realized I had a horse!"

She'd started 4-H the previous summer with Jon Boy, but used Chance as her project the second year. "We took first place in many 4-H horse show events and qualified to show in the State Fair (Blackfoot, Idaho). Chance and I didn't win much at State, but we went there several years and it was a lot of fun. Everybody had their horses clipped and groomed and were dressed fancier."

At home, however, she and Chance gathered more trophies every year. Heather and Chance really enjoyed the trail classes. He'd do everything right, and never hit the poles, and side-pass perfectly over to the mailbox. Michael said it was amusing to take an Arab to a pro-Quarter Horse show and see Heather win every class she entered. "Chance was very smart and level headed, and always calm and laid back. He had the endurance of an Arab, and could go all day, all summer long, and never get tired, but was as mellow as any kid horse," says Michael.

Chance was so versatile and accommodating that anyone could ride him. There were two boys in 4-H that liked to switch horses with Heather because they could do things with him that they couldn't do on their own horses. "Chance could be calm and cautious, but if you wanted him to go fast, he'd really go – and that's what the one kid liked about him because his own horse was lazy. The other kid's horse had been a steer-wrestling horse and was prancing and lively. He enjoyed riding Chance because he could get Chance to go slowly and be mellow. The three of us enjoyed clowning around before meetings; we'd play musical horses. Those boys started fighting over which one would get to ride Chance, and they wanted to ride him for different reasons, since he could do whatever the rider asked him," Heather says.

She also used him for roping. "He'd never been roped from before. I did a lot of roping off him in Working Ranch and he did fine, except for when I'd accidentally get the rope under his tail. It didn't bother him if it was a lead rope (if I was leading another horse) but he didn't like the stiff lariat. He'd clamp his tail so hard that I couldn't get it out. I could rope a cow or calf, or him, and get the rope around his legs or head and it was no big deal, but if it got under his tail I had a hard time getting it back. The class was judged on how many heads and heels you can catch in a certain length of time, and I'd lose time trying to get the rope out from under his tail!" she says.

"His best event was single cow penning. We had to sort out one cow and take her to designated spots around the arena, in a certain order, and hold her a few moments before moving her to the next place. Many contestants couldn't get their cows to pause long enough at the designated places. They got the cow too nervous and she'd be running around the arena," recalls Heather. Chance was so relaxed that this job was easy. He'd carefully move the cow around, and back off at just the right time so she wouldn't feel threatened or get excited, but put pressure on her to make her move when needed. He was very precise in his movements and reading the cow.

"This was humorous because a lot of the kids with their Quarter Horses couldn't get the job done! It frustrated them to see this little Arabian gelding very calmly and carefully maneuvering the cow. They'd usually beat us in team penning because it was fast action and some of the teams worked well together, but individually Chance was great at doing his thing. When it was one-on-one competition between Chance and the cow, we beat the Quarter Horses," recalls Heather.

Out on the range she could handle the cattle very well all by herself with Chance. He could quietly go through the cows to sort something out and never disturb the herd. "When we had cattle on our leased places and were moving some along a road, or helping neighbors move cattle, someone had to go through the herd to get ahead of the cows to guard a gate or a hole in a fence, without getting the cattle excited. I could do this on Chance, quietly going through to get ahead of them (without scaring them into running ahead of me), guard the hole until the herd got past, then do it again to get to the next place that needed to be blocked," says Heather.

"During 4-H years Chance could be just as mellow and slow as needed, but when I was ready for more advanced things, he'd take me to the next level. When we started rodeo events, we did it slowly. But as I got more confident he put in more speed. Even when we were doing wild, crazy things, I knew he'd take good care of me," she says.

"One time when we were helping another rancher move cows, the cattle were getting away from us and we had to run as fast as we could across the field to try to beat them to a gate. For a fat little Arabian he could actually run fast. We were going all out, and there was a hole he had to maneuver around and tossed his head a little to maintain his balance. The reins flipped and were both on the same side. I could still guide him with leg pressure and we kept going. When we needed to slow down I just leaned back a little and didn't have to pull on the reins – and then I was able to flip them back into place. He and I were a team and completely trusted each other. We could do anything together; he could practically read my mind," says Heather.

Chance also loved "people food." "He'd eat anything we offered him. Dad was riding him one spring, eating a chicken sandwich when he stopped for lunch. Chance was interested in it, so Dad fed him the rest of the sandwich! He was a carnivorous horse!"

One day she and Nick were doing chores and Chance ate the dog-food. "I always did the horse chores and Nick had to take care of the dogs. Nick was playing around, sword-fighting an imaginary

Molly and Chance

Young Heather roping on Chance at the working ranch class at the fair.

adversary, and left the dog-food bucket unattended. The horses were grazing around the house, and Chance found the bucket. He ate so much of it that Nick had to come back to the house to refill it to feed the dogs."

At the fairgrounds during a horse show, Heather, her mom and Chance were waiting for the next class. "A little girl with a plate of warm nachos walked in front of us, and Chance thought the food was for him. He stuck his nose into her plate. The poor girl was scared to death; she dropped her plate and ran. Chance looked at her as she ran away, as if to say, 'Wow. That's strange!' and then put his head down and started eating the nachos. Mom and I took the plate away from him, because the nacho cheese was getting all over his pretty, white nose and he was about to go into the show ring. We felt bad he scared that little girl, but all he wanted was her food, and thought she was serving it to him," recalls Heather.

The whole family rode him at various times. I rode him once, when Michael and Carolyn trailered horses to round up an orphan calf at one of their leased places. Young Heather had injured her knee playing basketball and couldn't ride. A cow had got on her back in a ditch and died, so we had to get her calf into the corral to haul home. We found the calf and brought him with some cows through the brush and ditches to get to the corral, and Chance did an excellent job for me on that roundup.

Chance didn't start showing his age until he was 25. As his joints became stiff, he was turned out to pasture. Young Heather was busy training horses for other people by then. Toward the end of his second summer of retirement (after Heather went to college), he suffered a severe wire cut on a front foot. Michael and Carolyn suspected that the dogs on that leased place chased him into a fence. Carolyn had to treat and bandage the wound daily for several weeks. She never had to put a halter on him; she'd just go out with the supplies to clean the wound and change his bandage and he'd stand patiently, even when the medicine stung. The wound healed and he was no longer lame, but it damaged the coronary band near his heel and his foot grew lopsided.

By that time Chance and Molly were retired, spending their remaining years at pasture. They'd been best buddies since Chance arrived at the ranch. Even if there were other horses in the pasture, Molly and Chance were off by themselves as a herd of two. When Chance started to lose vision, Molly kept track of him. He was perfectly happy as long as he was with her and knew where she was.

But for awhile they were separated. The first year Heather went to college (Carroll College in Helena, Montana) in the fall

Magpie helping Chance eat his breakfast.

of 2009 Chance became thin that winter. His teeth were bad and he had trouble eating hay. Michael and Carolyn brought him to our place early the next spring because they didn't have green grass yet on their leased place. In his skinny condition he'd developed some kind of skin problem, with hair loss.

I rotated him around in various pens that had green grass, and fed him a mix of grain, senior pellets and alfalfa pellets. Within a few months he was gaining weight and looking better. His hair grew back and he looked like a younger horse. He spent the next winter with us also. One of the local magpies adopted Chance, eating grain out of the tub with him and cleaning up any that spilled on the ground. In the early mornings Chance waited for his grain with his pet magpie; the sassy bird would be perched on his back as they waited for breakfast. Heather came to visit when she was home for Thanksgiving and Christmas. Chance loved it when she rubbed and tickled him. He was always excited to see her.

During the latter part of the second winter, he lived in our back yard because we needed all the pens for calving. Even though he was getting adequate nutrition from the senior pellets, he craved more roughage and started chewing fences. He couldn't eat hay because of his bad teeth, so I started "chewing" some hay for him. I selected the finest-stemmed grass hay, and snipped it into inch-long segments with scissors. It only took about 10 minutes morning and evening to snip enough to fill a two-gallon bucket, and he could eat that without having to chew it much.

Michael and Carolyn wintered all their horses in one of our pastures that year, and fed them big round bales in bale feeders. Molly (a year older than Chance) started to lose weight. Lynn and I brought her down to our corral to feed her separately and add some grain to her diet.

Chance was in the back yard, across the creek, and when we brought Molly to the corral, he was so excited! He'd been content to live by himself, but missed his old friend. When he heard her whinny, he ran around whinnying all afternoon and that first night. Then he settled down and was content to see glimpses of her through the trees along the creek.

After Heather got home from college for the summer, she and Nick took the two old horses to their place to graze around their house and barnyard, where Heather could feed them senior pellets and alfalfa pellets to help maintain their weight. They hauled the horses to the vet to have their teeth floated, but Chance still had trouble eating hay.

The last two years of his life, it was harder to keep weight on the old gelding. He had a lump behind his jaw and it became larger. "It didn't affect his swallowing, but may have been the reason he lost weight so dramatically. If it was cancer, it was probably eating him from the inside out. He still had lots of enthusiasm, and was frisky, but slowly starving to death in spite of all the special feed we gave him," recalls Heather.

By late fall 2012, it was obvious that Molly and Chance were nearing the end of their days. They would have a hard time getting through another winter. The family started making plans to put them down. Then they went out on a cold day to evaluate those old horses. It was hard to say goodbye, and they were both frisky and feeling good, still enjoying life. "They changed our minds!" recalls Heather. "Chance was so excited to see me, so feisty and full of life.

One of his favorite games was a tickle fight. I'd tickle his belly by his flank and he'd swing his head around and pretend he was going to bite me (but he never did). He loved the attention and this is something he and I had always done – mock teasing like he might do with a pasture buddy. When I tickled him that day he was playing our old game. We elected to baby them through one more winter, so they could have another good summer together."

So that winter Chance and Molly lived in the corral near their house, and Carolyn took care of them while Heather and Nick were in college and Michael was in North Dakota driving trucks. Carolyn fed their mush morning and night, and blanketed them at night. Chance was getting a lot of grain and special feeds but was very thin. He hadn't bounced back during summer like he usually did, and went into winter thin – and needed a warm, heavy blanket.

It was a chore for Carolyn to take care of those elderly horses – blanketing them at night, taking the blankets off during sunny hours of the day, feeding pellets soaked with water to make their food easier to eat. This was a labor of love. She worked part time in town at a veterinary clinic, and on bitterly cold days when she had to leave for work before sunup, we drove up later in the morning to take off their blankets.

Molly and Chance were happy together that winter, and when green grass came they went out on pasture again – and had one more good summer. Heather brought them down to our place in June and we pastured them along a driveway and ditch banks, and grazed off the haystack yard before we stacked hay. Every day, she came down to change their fly masks and feed their mush, patiently waiting for Chance to eat his (it took him three times as long as Molly).

"Chance was always happy to see me and his food, and do his eager little dance. I used a big tub because it took him a long time to eat and he dribbled a lot, and didn't waste as much with the big tub. He was never pushy, always polite, but he'd stand two inches away from me as I gave him his food, impatiently doing his dance. I'd have to wait there, to make sure Molly didn't come finish it for him (because she ate faster).

"It was inconvenient and time consuming to sit and wait for an hour, but we had a lot of quality time together. It took them a long time to shed out so I'd groom them and comb their manes and tails. Sure, I could have been doing other things, but it was time that I got to have with those old horses." That last summer was a gift to them, and to Heather, with good memories.

Chance and Molly had that summer together enjoying one another's company, but it was definitely time to let them go before cold weather. They were both thin, with very little flesh covering for

Chance in 2011 – still fat and sassy at age 27.

insulation, and Chance was losing his sight. Michael was home for a few days in early October from his North Dakota job driving trucks, and the timing was right. He took on the unpleasant but necessary task of giving those old horses the final kindness, honor and respect they deserved – a swift and painless death (one bullet to the forehead as he held onto the halter) – releasing them from the discomfort and infirmities of failing bodies. It was a beautiful fall day, and the family selected a final resting place along a meadow. They are buried there, overlooking the meadow and creek bottom where they spent many happy hours together.

"I'm sure it was hard for Heather to say goodbye to Chance," says Michael. "He was the first horse of her own, and the first she's had to put down. But she was very grown up about it. I asked her if she wanted to leave, in the final moments, but she didn't. She just stepped back and allowed me to give him a swift and painless release – from a life that had become a burden to his failing body."

"I feel that prolonging life of a beloved animal is our selfishness," says Michael. "To be fair to the suffering animal, you have to let it go. There's a point where you need to make that decision, and it can be hard when we are emotionally attached. We want to keep them longer, for our own emotional needs."

Those last months with the old horses – whether it was Carolyn taking care of them their last winter, or young Heather patiently devoting part of her day to feed them extra during the summer – was an opportunity to have time with them and remember all the good times, and come to a point where it was easier to say goodbye.

"This gives a person time to reflect on all the things that make a good horse more than a horse. You remember all the reasons you put them through those final years of retirement, because they truly earned it," Michael says.

"Some people might feel that burying them was frivolous – that we should have put them out where the coyotes could recycle them. But burying them was our human way of honoring them, in a place where no one would build a house or a road in the future. There was a huge rock nearby, and I placed it over their grave with the backhoe. Marking the grave was something I did for Carolyn, Heather and Nick because those horses meant so much to them," he says.

Nick was in college in Iowa at the time, and his biggest regret was that he wasn't home, and didn't have a chance to tell Molly goodbye. Michael had the toughest job, putting them down, along with Andrea's two old horses (Snickers and Fozzy), the day before. As a family, we said goodbye to four horses that had meant a lot to us, and paid them tribute as we comforted one another in our loss.

www.ingramcontent.com/pod-product-compliance
Lightning Source LLC
Chambersburg PA
CBHW040136270326
41927CB00020B/3412